Storyteller's Sampler

STORYTELLER'S SAMPLER

TALES FROM TELLERS AROUND THE WORLD

MARGARET READ MACDONALD, EDITOR

 LIBRARIES UNLIMITED™

An Imprint of ABC-CLIO, LLC

Santa Barbara, California • Denver, Colorado

Library of Congress Cataloging-in-Publication Data

Storyteller's sampler : tales from tellers around the world / Margaret Read MacDonald, editor.
     pages cm.
  Includes bibliographical references and index.
  ISBN 978-1-4408-3527-8 (pbk : acid-free paper)—ISBN 978-1-4408-3528-5 (ebook) 1. Tales.
2. Storytelling. 3. Children's libraries—Activity programs. I. MacDonald, Margaret Read, 1940– editor.
  GR76.S75 2015
  398.2—dc23   2015004316

ISBN: 978-1-4408-3527-8
EISBN: 978-1-4408-3528-5

19 18 17 16 15 1 2 3 4 5

This book is also available on the World Wide Web as an eBook.
Visit www.abc-clio.com for details.

Libraries Unlimited
An Imprint of ABC-CLIO, LLC

ABC-CLIO, LLC
130 Cremona Drive, P.O. Box 1911
Santa Barbara, California 93116-1911

This book is printed on acid-free paper ∞
Manufactured in the United States of America

CONTENTS

MALAYSIA

MEXICO

MONGOLIA

NEPAL

NETHERLANDS

PHILIPPINES

POLAND

RUSSIA

SAUDI ARABIA

SIBERIA

SOUTH AMERICA

THAILAND

UKRAINE

INTRODUCTION

We are pleased to present a special selection of 54 tales from the World Folklore Series that have been published over the years by Libraries Unlimited. The 40 collections in that series have done an amazing service by presenting world folktales for our child readers and for use by teachers in our classrooms. Under the guidance of editor Barbara Ittner, storytellers and educators from many countries were persuaded to collect tales and prepare collections.

Not every library can house the entire collection, so it was decided that a collection of especially tellable tales from the series could be useful. We have added a few simple activities to expand each story. We think you will have fun sharing these with your children.

Many of these collections were prepared by authors who were storytellers themselves, so we are able to present tales in the voice of the storyteller. To enhance your use of the stories, we provide information about the storytellers who shared the tales.

We hope you will want to take a look at the collections from which these tales come and read more. Each collection contains around 35 tales. This compilation includes favorite stories from 30 of the 40 collections. For more wonderful stories, see the list of all titles in the Libraries Unlimited World Folklore Series on page 175. Each of these books includes background information about the country along with recipes and games to accompany your unit of study. The books in this series provide a useful introduction to country studies as well as an engaging set of tales to share.

We hope this *Storyteller's Sampler* leads you to the collections in the World Folklore Series on a search for even more great tales to share!

ARMENIA

From *The Flower of Paradise and Other Armenian Tales* by Bonnie C. Marshall. Edited by Virginia Tashjian. (Libraries Unlimited, 2007).

KNOW-IT-ALL TANGIK
Pronounced Taneek

Dolma is an Armenian national dish that consists of grape leaves or vegetables stuffed with ground meat, spices, and rice or bulgur (cracked wheat).

There once lived a woman named Tangik. Whatever was said to her, she answered, "I know, I know!"

One day before leaving for the field, Tangik's husband said to his wife, "I'd like to have a taste of *dolma*. I haven't eaten any *dolma* for a long time."

Know-It-All Tangik didn't know how to prepare *dolma*, so she had to go to Tello, her neighbor, to ask for help.

"*Akhchi* (Miss) Tello, how is *dolma* prepared?"

"First you have to cut up the meat," Tello began explaining.

"I know!" Tangik hurried to answer with great dignity.

"Then you must put the meat in a copper saucepan."

"I know."

"Add a little salt and pepper."

"I know, I know."

"Cut up some onion finely. Add some coriander and mint . . . "

"I know, I know."

"Stuff grape leaves with the mixture and then roll them up. Put the rolls in a copper saucepan."

"I know, I know."

"Well, since you know everything already, do it your way. Why did you come to me pretending not to know anything?" Tello asked angrily.

"Is anything else needed? Is that all?" Tangik asked cautiously. Then Tangik decided that she would prepare such tasty *dolma* that her husband would lick his fingers in satisfaction.

Tello noted that Tangik had too high an opinion of herself, so Tello said, "There is one more thing. Take a piece of dry dung and put it into the saucepan on top of the *dolma*. Let it stew well."

Tangik couldn't contain herself and said, "I know, I know. I already know."

Tangik left to prepare the *dolma*. Tello cried after her. "When the smell of dung fills the air, you'll know that the *dolma* is ready."

PLAYING WITH THIS STORY

Snack on dolmathes. These are a bit tricky to make, though you can find recipes online. They are available ready-made from Trader Joe's and other specialty stores. Cut them in smaller pieces for your snacks.

ABOUT THIS STORY

Know-it-alls are disliked in any culture. The Native American teller Jonny Moses tells a spunky tale about Crow being slowly grabbed by Miss Octopus, one tentacle at a time. Every time she speaks to him, he sasses back, "I know!" It can be heard on his CD *American Indian Voices* (http://www.johnnymoses.com).

For another know-it-all, see the Indonesian story of "Why Shrimps Are Crooked" on page 67.

THE CUSTOMER AND THE HATTER

Acustomer once went to a hatter with a piece of sheepskin. "Make me a hat from this piece of sheepskin," he commanded.

"All right," said the hatter. "I'll make you a hat."

After leaving the shop, the customer began thinking. "That piece of sheepskin is big. Maybe the hatter could cut out two hats, instead of one."

The customer thought long and hard about the matter and returned to the hatter. "Tell me, hatter," he said. "Could you cut two hats out of that piece of sheepskin?"

"Why not? Of course I could," answered the hatter.

"If you could, then sew two hats," the customer said. Then he left.

The customer walked on for a while, and then he started thinking again. He returned to the hatter and asked, "Hatter, could you perhaps sew three hats from that piece of sheepskin?"

"Why not?" the hatter replied. "I'll sew three."

The customer was overjoyed. Pushing his luck, he asked, "Could you perhaps sew four hats?"

"I'll sew four hats for you," answered the hatter.

"What about five?"

"Yes, I can sew five hats."

"Then sew five hats for me."

The customer left but returned again after getting only halfway home.

"Hatter, could you perhaps sew six hats?"

"I could sew six hats."

"Could you sew seven? Or perhaps you could sew eight hats?"

"Well, why not? I could sew eight hats," said the hatter.

"Then sew eight hats for me."

"Very well, I'll sew eight hats. Come get your order in a week."

After a week had passed, the customer went to the hatter to get his order. "Are my hats ready?" he asked.

"They're ready," the hatter answered. He called to his apprentice and said, "Go bring this customer his hats."

The apprentice came immediately, carrying eight little hats. None of them would fit onto a head, but they might fit onto an apple.

The customer looked at them in amazement. "What's this?" he asked.

"These are the hats you ordered," replied the hatter.

"But why are they so small?"

"Take a moment to think about it, and see if you can come up with the answer," said the hatter.

The customer took the eight little hats and left. Puzzled, the customer started thinking. "Why are these hats so small? Why?"

Do you know the answer?

PLAY WITH THIS STORY

Cut out hats. Pass out sheets of paper and hat cutouts of various sizes. Let the children decide how many hats, and of what size, they can cut out of their paper. They trace the hat cutouts, cut out their hats, and decorate them. How many chose to make big hats, but only a few? How many chose to make many hats, but small ones?

Compare with Similar Tales

Share these picture books and discuss. *Something from Nothing* by Phoebe Gilman (New York: Scholastic, 1993). *Bit by Bit* by Steve Sanfield, illustrated by Susan Gaber (New York: Orchard, 1991). *Joseph Had a Little Overcoat* by Simms Taback (New York: Viking, 1999).

ABOUT THIS STORY

This is an unusual tale. It is somewhat similar to Motif J1115.4.1 *Tailor Makes Vest from Worn Out Coat*. In that story, a tailor makes ever smaller items from worn-out pieces: coat, vest, hat,

and a button. It ends with the tailor having "just enough to make a story." Find this story in *Earth Care: World Folktales to Talk About* by Margaret Read MacDonald (Atlanta: August House, 2005), pp. 94–97; in *Three-Minute Tales* by Margaret Read MacDonald (Atlanta: August House, 2004), pp. 52–54; and in the picture books cited above.

ABOUT THE AUTHORS

Bonnie C. Marshall is a Russian scholar and teacher for the New Hampshire Historical Society. She worked with Armenian storyteller and librarian Virginia A. Tashjian in preparing this book. Virginia was fluent in Armenian and active in the Armenian Church. She dedicated much of her life to passing on the Armenian language, culture, and values to her family and community.

AUSTRALIA

From *Gadi Mirrabooka: Australian Aboriginal Tales from the Dreaming*. Retold by Pauline E. McLeod, Francis Firebrace Jones, and June E. Barker. Edited by Helen F. McKay (Libraries Unlimited, 2001).

TIDALICK

A Story from the Murray River Region of New South Wales

Retold in Gadi Mirrabooka *with permission by Pauline E. McLeod.*

When the world was young, Tidalick, the little frog, became very thirsty. He began to drink all the water in a nearby river and drank and drank and drank.

Tidalick soon drank all the water that was in the river, and he *grew* and *grew* and *grew* and *grew, longer* and *longer* and *longer*, as he continued to drink all the water throughout the land.

He drank the streams and then the rivers, the billabongs, lagoons, waterholes, and all the waterways. It was not long before all the water was in Tidalick's enormous stomach and the land became parched and dry.

A great drought spread throughout the land. All the creatures, both of the land and of the water, suffered a terrible thirst. Trees withered, the land dried and cracked, and all the creatures suffered.

When they found out that the drought was caused by the greed of Tidalick, the giant frog, the creatures held a meeting to decide how to get Tidalick to open his mouth and share some of the water.

It was agreed that a group should go to Tidalick, the greedy frog, and ask him to share some of the water with others. Kangaroo, Dingo, Goanna, and Emu went together to see Tidalick. They asked him if he would open his mouth and share the water, as everyone was so very thirsty.

But Tidalick refused. He tightly closed his mouth, and not a drop of water came out.

The creatures held another meeting to discuss how they could get Tidalick to open his mouth so the water could come out. It was decided that if they could make Tidalick laugh, then the water would escape.

So all the different creatures from throughout the land gathered to where Tidalick, the giant frog, sat bloated and full of all the water from throughout the land.

A procession of kangaroos jumped in line, one after the other, followed by incredible leaps and bounds that had all the animals opening their mouths in amusement and wonder. They played leap the frog, and all the creatures laughed.

Not Tidalick! He just sat there. Not a smile, not a grin, and not one drop of water left his mouth.

The next creatures to try were the tall emus, with their long legs and long necks. When they danced in formation in front of Tidalick, their dance routine had all the animals opening their mouths in amazement and wonder. One emu got all tangled up and tripped over his legs, and all the creatures laughed.

But not Tidalick! He just sat there. Not a smile, not a grin, and not one drop of water left his mouth.

Next came the wobbly wombats. With their short legs and fat, round bodies, they wobbled, one after the other, from side to side, in a long line, quick wobbles and slow wobbles that had all the animals opening their mouths in amazement and wonder. Then one wombat wobbled the wrong way, and all the creatures laughed.

But not Tidalick! He just sat there. Not a smile, not a grin, and not one drop of water left his mouth.

The next creature to try was the kookaburra. He knew so many great jokes that even he laughed out loud.

But not Tidalick! He just sat there. Not a smile, not a grin, and not one drop of water left his mouth.

In the audience was an eel, who had lost his watery home to Tidalick, the greedy frog. The eel became so upset and angry that Tidalick would not share the water and give back his home that he slithered in front of Tidalick and began to tell him off. So upset was the eel that he became all twisted and knotted up. He looked so funny!

Suddenly, Tidalick grinned. He smiled a big smile. Then he started to titter. You see, Tidalick had never seen an eel so angry and twisted and all knotted up before. It looked so funny, he began to laugh.

His laughter quickly became a big belly laugh, and before long the water began gushing out of Tidalick's mouth, filling the streams, rivers, billlabongs, lagoons, waterholes, and all the waterways across the land.

Eel was so happy that his home was back that he unknotted himself and quickly slithered right back into his watery habitat.

Tidalick became smaller and smaller, as gallons of water poured out of him, until finally he became the size that frogs are today.

The animals decided that Tidalick would never again be allowed to cause another great drought through his greed as he did in the First Time, when the world was young.

TELLING THIS STORY

It is fun to ask the children to drink up the water and make big cheeks, as if their mouths are full of water. Ask them after each animal tries to make Tidalick laugh, "Do you think he laughed?" They will shake their heads. When it is the eel's turn, make it clear that he is the really funny one who is going to win. Then have them all open their mouths to let the pretend water rush out.

PLAY WITH THIS STORY

Act this story out. Let one child be Tidalick. Then have the other children take turns trying to make him or her laugh. Choose a very lithe child to be the eel who twists into knots to finally make Tidalick laugh.

ABOUT THIS STORY

A1111. *Impounded water. Water is kept by monster so that mankind cannot use it.*

Several Native American stories tell of water hoarding. MacDonald and Sturm's *Storyteller's Sourcebook* cites versions from Tlingit and Passamaquody traditions. A Haitian tale, "Papa God's Well," in *Earth Care: World Folktales to Talk About* by Margaret Read MacDonald (Atlanta: August House, 2005), pp. 52–56, tells of a frog refusing to let anyone drink from the well.

W155.5. *Permission to drink from water tank.*

The motif of making the monster laugh to release the water is unusual.

FROG AND THE LYREBIRD
A Story from the People
of the Blue Mountains

Retold with permission by Pauline E. McLeod.

In the days long ago, a stream fed from the Blue Mountains into the Murray River. As we know, all streams have bubbles in them. But in this stream, the bubbles were ALIVE. They were the little crystal homes of Water Spirits.

There was one little Water Spirit who wanted to be free so it could dance and play with all the other creatures. It wished, and wished, and wished. It wished so much that it turned into a little green creature. But it still could not escape from its crystal home.

The Lyrebird would come down to the stream every day to have a drink. It was used to seeing all the bubbles. But on this one day in spring, it noticed that one of the bubbles was green. So it sang to it, and the little green bubble danced to the Lyrebird's music. It dived deep into the waters and came out with a magical splash, and dived again and again, for quite some time.

Eventually, the Lyrebird became bored and was about to go home, when the Great Spirit spoke to him, saying, "Lyrebird! Lyrebird! Go back to the little green bubble and sing to it. One of my creatures wants to be free. Only your voice can set it free. Go on, Lyrebird, go back and sing!"

Feeling very important, the Lyrebird went back to the little green bubble and started to sing. He sang and sang and sang. He sang until he was about to burst, then he sang some more.

Suddenly, the bubble popped! Out jumped a Little Green Frog. He opened his mouth, but nothing came out. Not a whisper; not a sound.

"Oh!" said the Lyrebird." Everything makes a sound. Try again."

The Little Green Frog tried. It opened its mouth once again, but still nothing came out. Not a whisper, not even a tiny sound.

"Ha!" said the Lyrebird in disgust.

He was about to go home, when the Great Spirit spoke again. "Lyrebird! Lyrebird! Go back to the Little Green Frog and teach him how to sing. He'll be a good student. He will listen and learn. I know you will be a good teacher. Go on, teach him how to sing."

So, feeling very important, Lyrebird went back to teach the Little Green Frog.

Day after day, season after season, the Lyrebird would go down to the stream to teach the Little Green Frog how to sing, and the Little Green Frog would always be there to listen and to learn.

One day, the Little Green Frog decided to play a trick on the Lyrebird. So the Little Green Frog hid from the Lyrebird.

The Lyrebird went down to the stream as he had done so many times before and was very surprised. The Little Green Frog was nowhere to be seen.

The Lyrebird searched everywhere for the Little Green Frog but could not find him anywhere. Just when the Lyrebird had decided to give up and go home, he heard his brother calling him. He turned but could not see anyone.

The Lyrebird heard his brother's voice again and turned. This time he saw where the Little Green Frog was hiding. The frog was laughing.

"So you have learnt to throw your voice, have you?" said the Lyrebird. "That is good. For it is time for you to be heard by everyone else."

The Lyrebird was so proud of his student that he forgot all about his own singing and called out to all the creatures, "Come! Come and listen to the Little Green Frog!

That night, when the moon was high, all the animals, all the birds, and all the other creatures gathered around the stream. But there was no Little Green Frog to be seen. He was fast asleep. The Lyrebird knew that when the Little Green Frog sleeps, he sleeps with all the other Water Spirits.

So the Lyrebird went to the water's edge and called out, "Little Green Frog, wake up! They are all here, waiting for you."

Before long, the bulging eyes of the Little Green Frog appeared in the water. He jumped up onto his lily pad and puffed out his chest.

When all the animals, all the birds, and all the other creatures saw him, they laughed and said, "What is this, Lyrebird? You asked us here to look at this strange little creature that looks like a bloated green man?"

"No!" said the Lyrebird, "You are not here to look at him; you are here to listen!"

Throughout that night, the music that came from the Little Green Frog was magical. The songs he sang contained all the sounds of all the other animals. He finally made the most beautiful sound of all, the sound of rain landing on hard, dry, parched earth.

When the Little Green Frog finished and all the animals, all the birds, and all the other creatures had returned home, the Lyrebird went over to his student and said, "I am so proud of you! You sing better than I do."

When he said that, the Little Green Frog became so embarrassed. He dived deep into the water of the stream and waited until the Lyrebird had gone home.

Then he jumped up on his favorite lily pad, puffed out his chest, and said, "I am the greatest singer in the whole world! I sing better than the Lyrebird!"

The Little Green Frog was very lonely, all by himself in the stream, so the Great Spirit created another frog to be his wife.

"I am the greatest singer in the whole wide world!" boasted the Little Green Frog to his wife. "If I wanted to, I could sing the moon down from the sky."

"Go on. I dare you!" said his wife. "Go ahead and try!"

So the Little Green Frog sat on his lily pad, puffed out his chest, and sang and sang and sang. He sang until he was about to burst. Then he sang some more.

But the moon just sailed right on by. It didn't listen to a note.

But that Little Green Frog would not give up, and he tried again. He sang and he sang and he sang. He sang until he was about to burst. Then he sang some more.

Suddenly, his voice went "CROAK!" And that is the only sound that came out of his mouth.

From that day to this, the only song all the Little Green Frogs are able to sing is "CROAK, CROAK, CROAK."

But men, women, and children still love listening to the Lyrebird, the patient teacher of the Little Green Frog. That is the reason why frogs croak and the Lyrebird sings.

TELLING THIS STORY

Find a picture of a lyrebird to show the children before the story. This is a very unusual bird, so having an image in mind helps.

PLAY WITH THIS STORY

Sing and play a frog voice song. Cut circles about 4 inches in diameter from stiff green poster board. Fold each over in the middle. Stick Avery dots to the top of the fold for eyes. Put a rubber band around the folded circle between the eyes. Open the frog's mouth (the folded circle) with your hand and strum the rubber band to make it sing

To sing this song, you need to make a catching noise in your throat on the "Glack . . . GOONG!" Blink your eyes rapidly when you sing, "And his eyes went Glack . . . glack . . . GOONG!"

Jump to lily pads. Cut large lily pads from green paper and strew them on the floor. Sing your Glack-goong song and jump onto a new lily pad each time you sing "Glack-goong."

LITTLE GREEN FROG

MRM

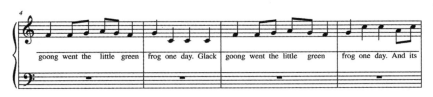

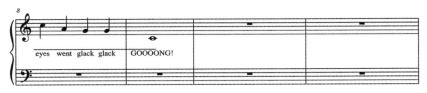

ABOUT THIS STORY

A2426.4.1. *Frog's croak.*

This is an Aboriginal story from the people living in the Blue Mountains in New South Wales, Australia.

ABOUT THE STORYTELLER

PAULINE E. MCLEOD began sharing her culture with children and educators in 1990 and worked with schools throughout New South Wales. She also lectured in Aboriginal Studies at TAFE (technical and further education) colleges. She told her tales on *Playschool* and other Australian television programs.

Pauline was one of the "stolen generation," taken from her family at the age of two and give to a Caucasian family to raise. As an adult, Pauline reconnected with her Monaro and Ngarrindjeri people. She performed at reconciliation forums throughout Sydney from 1996 to 2000. Sadly, she passed away in 2003. For the stories she contributed to *Gadi Mirrabooka*, Pauline had visited her tribal elders to ask permission for the stories to be included in this book for use by non-Aboriginal tellers. Aboriginal tales cannot be used by non-Aboriginal tellers without such permission.

HELEN MCKAY, founder and life member of Australian Storytelling Guild (NSW) Inc., is author of *Gadi Mirrabooka* and *Links to Your Happiness* plus *The Happy Book*. With coauthor Berice Dudley, she wrote *About Storytelling* and *Riotous Riddles*. Currently a studio potter, Helen was formerly a ceramic artist and teacher of three-dimensional art in secondary schools.

In an attempt to save their traditional stories for future generations of Australians, three Aboriginal story custodians assisted Helen by telling a selection of their indigenous stories in *Gadi Mirrabooka*, a book of 33 Aboriginal stories.

Helen's Web site is http://www.helenmckay.com.

BRAZIL

Brazilian Folktales by Livia de Almeida and Ana Portella. Edited by Margaret Read MacDonald, (Libraries Unlimited, 2006).

THE OLD LADY AND THE MONKEY

Once upon a time there lived an old lady who had plenty of banana trees in her backyard. They were so plentiful that the woman managed to prepare all kinds of sweets with the fruits, and she became heavier and heavier. Finally she was so fat that she couldn't climb up the wooden ladder to get the bananas. As she looked up at the sweet fruits, she had an idea. She would call Monkey to help. Monkey could easily climb up the banana trees and get her the bananas.

Monkey came and quickly climbed to the top of the banana tree. The old lady shouted, "Good, Monkey, now you can pick the fruits and throw them here in my basket!"

But Monkey had different plans. He began to eat the best fruit and throw the rotten and the green bananas. The old lady had not even one good banana to eat. She was furious, and prepared her revenge.

On the next day, she made a tar doll and dressed it as a girl. She even put red ribbons on the fake doll's hair. She let the doll stand by the door of her house with a basket full of ripe bananas. Soon enough Monkey showed up and asked the girl to give him a banana.

"Girl, give me a banana!"

But the tar doll would not answer. Monkey insisted. Nothing. Monkey got angry and warned, "Hey, girl, give me a banana or I will slap your face."

No answer.

Monkey slapped the doll's face and got caught by the tar.

Monkey became nervous.

"Let me go, otherwise, I will slap you with my other hand."

No answer.

Monkey slapped the doll again. His other hand also got caught.

"Let me go or I will kick you!"

No answer.

Monkey kicked the doll again. His foot got caught.

"Let me go or I will kick you with my other foot!"

No answer.

Monkey kicked the doll again. His foot got caught again.

"Let me go or I will whip you with my tail!"

No answer.

Monkey whipped the doll with his tail and got caught.

Now Monkey was completely stuck on the tar doll.

The old woman came from her hiding place inside the house with a big knife. "I will have Monkey stew for dinner!" she chortled.

And that is just what she made. She killed the Monkey and started to prepare the meat for dinner.

But a voice could be heard singing,

"Stew me gently, stew me slow. If you change your mind, let me go."

The old lady ignored the singing voice. She put spices, vegetables, and chopped monkey into a pan and began to cook her stew.

Then she heard, "Cook me gently, cook me slow. If you change your mind, let me go."

When the stew was ready, the old lady sat down and ate with great appetite. While she ate, she could still hear a voice singing.

"Eat me gently, eat me slow. If you change your mind, let me go."

After that feast, the old lady felt really sleepy. She decided to take a siesta. She woke soon feeling really sick. Her belly was swollen as if she were pregnant. And inside her stomach a voice was singing.

"Digest me gently. Digest me slow. Listen to me! You'd better let me go!"

"All right! All right! GO!"

Then the old lady's belly started swelling. It got bigger and bigger and bigger.

Suddenly . . . it exploded!

Out flew dozens of little monkeys, who all jumped up singing, dancing, and making faces at the old woman.

"One monkey cooked gently, one monkey cooked slow . . . makes many, many monkeys! Good-bye! We've got to go!"

PLAY WITH THIS STORY

Act out the story with a clay doll and a monkey. Give each child a small piece of Plasticine or modeling clay to make a little doll. With three pipe cleaners, form a monkey. Pipe cleaner #1: fold top fourth over into a circle to make a head. Pipe cleaner #2: wrap this around just under the head to make arms. Pipe cleaner #3: roll the bottom of pipe cleaner #1 up around the middle of pipe cleaner #3 to hold it and pull down the ends of pipe cleaner #3 to make legs.

Stick your pipe-cleaner monkey to your clay doll, one appendage at a time! You can retell the monkey-sticking-to-doll part of the story as you do this.

Share Similar Stories

West African: *A Story, a Story* by Gail E. Haley (Aladdin, 1988). In this Caldecott Medal winner, Ananse the Spider man gets stuck on a gum doll. This is a great read-aloud book.

African American: See a retelling of the Joel Chandler Harris version in *Uncle Remus: The Complete Tales* by Julius Lester, illustrated by Gerry Pinkney (New York: Dial, 1999). This version attempts to modernize the offensive dialect in which the original stories were written. *All Stuck Up* by Linda Haywood, illustrated by Norman Chartier (New York: Random House, 1990), is an easy-to-read version. For a tellable version based on an African American tale from West Virginia, see "The Rabbit and the Well" in *Twenty Tellable Tales* by Margaret Read MacDonald (Chicago: American Library Association, 2004), pp. 126–141.

Mexican: *The Tale of Rabbit and Coyote* by Tony Johnston, illustrated by Tomie DePaola (New York: Puffin, 1998).

Russian: *Tomie de Paola's Favorite Nursery Tales* by Tomie de Paola (New York: Putnam, 1986), pp. 75–82. Straw ox is smeared with pitch to catch animals.

Another Brazilian version: "Sambele" in *The Singing Sack: 28 Song-stories from around the World* by Helen East (London: A & C Black, 1989), pp. 67–69. In this story, monkey is caught by a little girl, his tail is torn off, and the other monkeys mock him with a singing refrain at the end.

ABOUT THIS STORY

This is a variant of K741 *Capture by tar baby*. The story is best known as the Brer Rabbit African American version recorded by Joel Chandler Harris. *The Complete Tales of Uncle Remus* (Boston: Houghton Mifflin, 1955). In our Brazilian version, the story combines with MacDonald motif Z13.5 *Fish calls "Take me home," "cook me," "eat me." Eaten. "I got you now."* and Z49.3.1 *The Picaro Bird. Is caught, cooked, eaten, causes king to vomit.*

JAGUAR AND GOAT

Once upon a time, there lived in the forest a jaguar and a goat. Jaguar was tired of living in dirty caves among the woods. She decided it was time to build her own place. A house of her own, just like she had always dreamt, on a nice plot of land. So she started to search for the right spot. It wasn't very easy to find exactly what she had in mind; however, after a long day she found the perfect spot. "This is exactly what I always wanted: sunny, full of trees, with a creek where I can bathe when it is hot. It is just a matter of weeding and leveling the ground. It will be lots of work. But it will be worthwhile!"

And on the next day, Jaguar worked hard on the plot, cleaning the area, leveling the ground. It was already geting dark when she gathered her tools and left, happy with the results of a hard day's work. "Tomorrow I will start building my own house."

Meanwhile, Mister Goat, tired of living with the other twenty goats on a farm, decided to build a house for himself. Goat had always dreamt of living by himself, doing whatever he pleased. One day, he left the farm very early to search for the right spot where he could build his own house. After much searching, he found the perfect spot. "This is so nice! It is exactly what I always wanted, sunny, full of trees, with a creek where I can bathe when it is hot. And look at this, the terrain is already clean! I can start to build the house right away," thought the goat.

He started to work, cutting trees and chopping the wood. By midday, he was exhausted, but all the wood he would need for the house was cut and neatly piled. Goat left, as happy as he could be, to get some rest.

Just after Goat had left, Jaguar came back. For this was exactly the same plot where Jaguar had decided to build her house. She couldn't believe her eyes when she found all the wood she needed cut and piled. "This is a miracle. Fortune is helping me! Now I will have to raise the walls, but with this help from Above, my home will be ready very soon!" Jaguar worked and worked. She raised the walls and the floor of the house. And she sang and whistled as she worked. She only stopped when night fell. She was tired, but it had been worthwhile: the walls were smooth and shiny, and strong. Jaguar was so proud of herself. She picked up her tools and left to take her well-deserved rest.

On the next day, Goat woke up very early, before sunrise, and went back to work. When he got there, he could not believe his eyes. "Miracle, this must be a miracle! Fortune is helping me!" The walls and the floor of his house were ready. He would have only to build the roof. And he worked the whole morning, really excited. By lunchtime, he had finished the roof. He covered the house with leaves from a coconut tree, tied them tightly with a fine rope, and trimmed the edges, so it would look nice. He worked very carefully for he did not want any leaks in his new house. He stood for a long time admiring his own work. Now he had to build the windows and the front door. He was a bit worried. "Will I be able to do it? I am so weak and little. Will I be able to do it on my own?" But this was something to be dealt with on the next day. He was really exhausted. He picked up all his tools and went back to the farm to get some rest.

Jaguar arrived just after lunch, full of energy. She wanted to finish as soon as possible so she could move into her new house. But when she arrived at the spot, she couldn't believe her eyes. The roof was ready! She fell on her knees. "Fortune is really helping me. This is a true blessing!" she exclaimed. And she worked harder than ever. Strong as she was, she easily put two windows in place and prepared a sturdy front door. "It is ready!" she said proudly. The windows and the door opened and closed smoothly, without a sound. Jaguar even added handles and locks. But now she was tired. "I must get some rest, but tomorrow, I will paint my house. I think I will be able to move sooner than I thought," thought Jaguar. And she left happily.

Goat left the farm to work very early. When he got there, for a moment he thought he had gone to the wrong place. He could not believe his eyes. "Is this really my house? Two windows, a door, handles and locks! I can only thank fortune. This surely is an amazing miracle!" Now he had to paint the house. He decided to paint the house white, with blue windows and door. And he worked and he worked. But it was worthwhile. The house looked lovely. Goat was happy as he could be. "Tomorrow, I can move here. I will only bring my best things. A house like this deserves the best," and he hurried away, ready to prepare his belongings.

Jaguar just arrived after midday and found the house already painted. She couldn't believe her eyes. "What a beauty! And it is painted with blue and white, my favorite colors. Fortune is helping me!" she thought. And she decided to move in the next day.

On the next day very early, Goat picked all his belongings and left for his new house.

Very early, Jaguar picked her possessions and left the forest.

Goat and Jaguar met in the middle of the road.

"Where are you going carrying all these things, Mister Goat?" asked Jaguar.

"I am moving to my new house, Mistress Jaguar. And where are you going?" asked Goat, very curious.

"I have also built a house, and I am moving there right now," answered Jaguar, very proud of herself.

"So I believe we are going to be neighbors. My house is this beauty right here!" said Goat.

"You are wrong, Master Goat, this is MY house. I have weeded, cleaned the plot, raised the walls, put the windows and door in place," said Jaguar, very angrily.

"But I chopped the wood, did the roof really carefully, and painted the whole house. I kept thinking that Fortune was helping me all the while!" said Goat, enraged.

"I also thought this was a miracle," roared Jaguar.

"And what are we supposed to do now?"

The two animals stood in silence for a while. Jaguar spoke first.

"I believe we must live together, then. But I warn you: I have a terrible temper. If you ever see me frowning, get away from me. This means I am really angry," said Jaguar. She wanted the Goat to feel very frightened and give up the house.

Goat was really scared of sharing the house with Jaguar, but he did not want to give up. "OK, Jaguar. I have understood. But take care yourself. If you ever see me sneezing and scratching my beard, get away from me. This means I am enraged!" said he.

And time went by. Each animal tried to keep away from the other as much as possible. But after a week, in the middle of the night, Goat woke up and saw Jaguar standing in the living room, frowning. Nervously, he started to sneeze and scratch his beard. The two of them looked at each other full of fright. They didn't think twice. Goat jumped through one window. Jaguar jumped through the other window. And they hurried away, running as fast as they could. They were so scared that they are still running away from each other to this day.

TELLING THIS STORY

In the traditional version above, the animals flee from each other in the end. I prefer to end the story with them deciding to cooperate and live happily together ever after.

PLAY WITH THIS STORY

Build a house. Cut flannel board pieces for the parts of the house. Jaguar: put up long green strip of grass. Goat: pile up logs (brown pieces). Jaguar: move brown logs upright to make a house. Lay one across the bottom for the floor. Goat: put green pieces (palm fronds) on top for a roof. Jaguar: add windows and a door. Goat: add blue frames around the windows and white pieces to decorate the sides of the house.

Act it out. This is also a fun story to act out as a tandem tale. Let each character tell what his character is doing as each enters and pretends to build. Then they scream and run from each other in the end.

ABOUT THIS STORY

K1715.3.2* *Goat begins to build a house. Tiger finds foundation and adds to it. Each thinks god is helping with the work.*

This tale seems to be of African origin. MacDonald's *Storyteller's Sourcebook* cites sources for Haiti, Brazil, Galla (Somalia), Congo, Tanzania, and Swahili.

ABOUT THE STORYTELLER

LIVIA DE ALMEIDA is a journalist and editor in Rio de Janeiro. She heard stories from her grandfather almost every night when she was growing up, and in 1996, she formed a storytelling troupe with five friends, Mil e Umas. She has been involved in organization storytelling events in Rio and has traveled to the United States to perform in storytelling festivals. Photo shows Livia on left, with Margaret MacDonald.

ABOUT THE COAUTHOR

Ana Portella is also a member of Mil e Umas, telling stories with this group throughout the Rio area.

ABOUT THE EDITOR

Margaret Read MacDonald met Livia when she was invited to participate in a week of Tellabration storytelling events in Rio de Janeiro. She and Livia cooperated on storytelling projects both in Brazil and in the United States.

CROATIA

From *Tales from the Heart of the Balkans*. Retold by Bonnie C. Marshall. Edited by Vasa D. Mihailovich (Libraries Unlimited, 2001).

THE LITTLE SHEPHERD

Once upon a time in Istria, a little shepherd was grazing a herd of cows, a flock of sheep, and a few goats near the seashore.

It was afternoon, and the hot sun was beating down on the earth when the little shepherd came upon three beautiful girls sleeping in a green glen. They were *vilas*. (In the Balkans, fairies or nymphs with magical powers are called *vilas*.) They were indescribably beautiful and resembled one another so much that they looked like sisters. They lay quietly and were apparently sleeping very soundly.

The little shepherd did not give it a thought that they might be *vilas*. He assumed that they were ordinary girls who had lain down on the grass and had fallen asleep after becoming tired from strolling in the hot sun.

The sun will burn them, the boy thought. It's a pity for such pretty faces to be damaged. I must help them somehow.

He climbed a lime tree, broke off its leafy branches, and stuck them around the girls so that the sun's rays could not burn them anymore.

Soon afterward, the *vilas* awoke and got up. They pretended to be amazed and asked each other who had been so kind as to protect them from the sun's burning rays. Of course, they knew very well what had happened, for *vilas* never fall asleep. They just pretend to be sleeping. The *vilas* asked what had happened only in order to see whether the little shepherd would speak.

The little boy did not answer. He tried to run away because looking at the *vilas* hurt his eyes. The light from their glistening hair, which shone like gold, blinded him.

In an instant all three were beside him. He could not escape. They asked him what kind of reward he wanted for protecting them from the hot sun, but the boy dared not ask for anything.

They offered him a magic purse of money that would always be full of golden coins, but the little shepherd did not care at all about the magic purse. He was too young to know the value of money. Playing with the money and looking at it were boring. After all, he had

---

cows and sheep that were dearer to him than anything else on earth. Why would he want money?

When the *vilas* discovered that the animals were dearest to the boy's heart, they said, "When you drive the herd home this evening, you will hear the ringing of bells coming from the direction of the sea. You will hear big bells with deep voices and little bells with high-pitched voices, but don't look back to see what is happening behind you until you reach home."

After giving the little shepherd these strange instructions, the girls disappeared. Because of their odd behavior, the boy realized that they were indeed *vilas*.

The sun sank slowly into the sea, and the little shepherd began driving his herd home. The closer he came to his house, the louder was the clanging and ringing behind his back. He began singing and picking flowers for his mother to distract himself from the ringing bells.

Soon he was thinking about how good his dinner would taste when he arrived home after a hard day's work. Finally, he forgot about the *vilas* and what they had told him.

When he was halfway home, he became so curious about the ringing of the bells that he turned around to see who could be behind him driving so many cattle home from pasture. No one in his village owned enough cattle to make such a great clamor of cowbells.

To his amazement he saw a large number of sheep, cows, and goats coming out of the sea, following his herd. The instant he turned around, they stopped coming out of the sea onto land. Only those that were already on dry land followed him home.

Had the little shepherd not turned around, he would have had an enormous number of new animals to add to his herd. However, he was not greedy for more than he already had. In fact, he was quite satisfied with the gift of the *vilas*.

He had enough animals so that he could give them to his poorer neighbors. From then on, no one in the village was needy anymore. The villagers prospered, and everyone remembered with gratitude the little shepherd's kindness.

PLAY WITH THIS STORY

Act it out. Place a line of tape across the floor to demarcate the edge of the lake. Some of the children stand in the lake as cows and sheep. They ring bells loudly. A few other children play the part of shepherds. The shepherds come out of the lake and walk forward without looking back. The sheep and cattle ring loudly and call out, trying to make them look back, while they file out of the lake slowly one at a time. If any of the shepherds look back, the cattle in the pond stop and cannot come out now. Switch roles and play again.

ABOUT THIS STORY

This is related to F302.4.2.1 *Fairy comes into man's power when he steals her clothes*, though this tale lacks the motif of stealing the clothing (wings). MacDonald and Sturm cite a Welsh variant in which the fairy wife can bring as many cattle from the lake as she can count in one breath: F343.9 *Fairy gives man horse, cattle, etc.*

C311 *Tabu: looking back* is a universal folk motif. Stith Thompson cites variants from every continent.

ŠKRAT, THE WOOD GOBLIN

There once lived a peasant who suffered misfortune every year. He could not make ends meet, so he accumulated one debt after another. He became heavily indebted to his rich neighbor, who showed no mercy in demanding that he return the money he borrowed right away. Because the peasant could not return the money, the rich man took him to court.

Early in the evening of the day when the peasant's property was to be sold to pay his debt, the despondent man was taking a walk in the forest. There, a hunter, whom he did not know, approached him and asked directions. The peasant told the hunter which direction to take and walked along with him to show him the way.

As they walked, they conversed about this and that. Finally, the peasant confided in the hunter concerning his troubles.

"I will help you if you give me something in return," the stranger said to him.

"I'll give you whatever you want," answered the peasant.

"Good," said the hunter. "I'll give you a sack full of gold. You'll be able to pay off your entire debt and still have some money left over. But you must give me that which you have at home and know nothing about."

What could it be that I have at home and know nothing about? wondered the peasant. What could it be? To the stranger, he said, "Just take whatever it is, sir. Whatever will be, will be, but you must help me."

"Fine," the hunter agreed. He gave the peasant a sack of gold coins and said, "In seven years, at this same time and on this same spot, you will hand over to me that which you have promised."

The peasant was a little perplexed as to why the stranger had decided everything so quickly. He could not figure out what it was he had at home, so he got worried. "Is there a way I can get out of giving you what you demand?" he asked.

The stranger laughed and said, "There is. If you find out what my name is before the appointed day, you can keep both the gold coins and that which you have promised me."

Then the stranger vanished without a trace, and the peasant remained standing on the spot with a sack in his hand. He did not think very much about the deal he had made or about the mysterious stranger, but hurried home so that he could tell his wife about his great joy.

He entered the house and was shocked to see that in his absence a son had been born. When he had made the deal with the hunter, the peasant had not known that he had a son at home. Unwittingly, he had sold his son to the stranger.

After he understood what he had done, he worried, but did not lose hope. He had seven years to think up a way to save his son, seven years to inquire about the identity of the mysterious stranger.

The very next day he paid his debt to his neighbor. He still had plenty of money left over, as the stranger had promised. He managed the money well, and his possessions increased with each passing year. He built a new home. He had a great variety of crops, and his barns were loaded with an abundant harvest.

His son grew up healthy and strong. Moreover, all of his tenants liked him. Often, he would set his child on his lap and look at him for a long time. As he watched the boy, his heart grew heavier and heavier. He never told anyone how he had acquired his money.

The years passed—the first, the second, the third, the fourth, the fifth, and the sixth—until finally the seventh year came. As the day approached when he would have to give up his child to the menacing hunter, the peasant's mood worsened. His face became wrinkled because of his great worry. He avoided all friendships and roamed the forests alone.

Who was the stranger? He constantly racked his brain for answers. He inquired secretly throughout the entire country about the names of various hunters. He learned the names of many people, but the name he was searching for was not among them.

Finally, only three days remained—three days and then he had to give up his little son. The peasant left the house sadly and went into the forest. Darkness was falling when he came to the place where he had made a deal with the stranger seven years ago. Because of his great sorrow and concern, at first the miserable peasant did not notice where he was. Then it dawned on him that he was on the very spot where he had met the hunter. He was astonished by what he saw.

At the place where they had stood seven years ago, a stake was burning and a little man was hopping around it. He was dressed in a crimson coat and green pants. He wore green boots and a green cap. The peasant's mouth fell open. Without blinking an eye, he stared at the little monster.

The little man began singing with great joy.

> Ho, ho, ho,
> The peasant doesn't know
> That Škrat's my name;
> Wood goblining's my game.
> I'll take his son,
> And off I'll run.
> Ho, ho, ho!

The peasant heard everything the little man said, and he laughed to himself happily. Hey, little fellow, he thought to himself, if that is so, then now I know who you are. He turned around and went home.

For two days the peasant was in a very good mood. As he waited for the hunter to come, he went about his business as usual.

On the evening of the third day, the expected guest arrived. The family had just eaten supper and was still assembled. The hunter entered the door and approached the master of the house.

"Let's find out if you know who I am, boss."

"Oh, how could I fail to know the name of a wood goblin like you, Škrat!" the peasant shouted.

Quick as lightning, Škrat turned around and flew through the door in a rage. As he was leaving, he grabbed a corner of the house, and it broke off.

The peasant's son remained behind. The peasant's big, beautiful house remained, too, but not one bricklayer succeeded in restoring the corner that Škrat had broken off. To this day the house still stands with one corner missing.

PLAY WITH THIS STORY

Make a broken house. Provide cutout houses for the children to decorate. Have them tear off one corner when it is finished.

Compare to Similar Stories

Rumpelstiltskin, retold by Edith H. Tarcov, illustrated by Edward Gorey (Scholastic, 1973).
Rumpelstiltskin's Daughter by Diane Stanley (HarperCollins, 2002).
Tom Tit Tot: An English Folktale, illustrated by Eveline Ness (Aladdin, 1997).

ABOUT THIS STORY

This is related to the Grimm's Rumpelstiltskin tale, D2183 *Magic spinning* (type 500–501). MacDonald gives variants of that tale from England (*Tom Tit Tot*), France, Scotland, Ireland, and Denmark. Though this story lacks the spinning motif, it does have the same consequence: giving up a child if you cannot guess the name. N475 *Secret name overheard by eavesdropper.* C432.1 *Guessing name of supernatural creature gives power over him.*

ABOUT THE AUTHORS

BONNIE C. MARSHALL is adjunct instructor and curriculum coordinator for the Russian program at Johnson C. Smith University. She has done fieldwork in Russia collecting songs, *chastushki* (four-line folk lyrics), and anecdotes.

VASA D. MIHAILOVICH is professor emeritus of Slavic languages and literature at the University of North Carolina, Chapel Hill. He was born in Yugoslavia and has published six collections of poetry and short stories in Serbo-Croatian as well as many English language publications on Slavic and Serbian literature.

CUBA

From *From the Winds of Manguito: Cuban Folktales in English and Spanish. Desde los vientos de Manguito: Cuentos folklóricos de Cuba, en inglés y español* by Elvia Pérez (Libraries Unlimited, 2004).

THE HEADLESS DANCE

A story from the Cuban oral tradition collected by Samuel Feijoo, retold by Elvia Pérez. For a Spanish text of this story, see From the Winds of Manguito, *pp. 91–94.*

Because the world is the world, there is a devil. But not many people know what the devil has to do with *dancing*. Well then, it happened that when the world was new, the devil was married to *la diabla*. They had a little devil son, *el diablito*, and they all lived together at their house in the country. Of course this was not fun for the animals that lived there, because nobody wants to have the devil for a neighbor. But the worst problem was not his devilments, but the constant fighting between him and his wife. For anything big or small that happened in that house . . . they fought. From morning to night . . . they fought. In summer and winter . . . they fought. This was a real problem because with every fight, they would set the place on fire! And there were hardly any rivers left with water enough to put out such flames

This is why, one day, the animals held a secret meeting to try and solve this problem. It was not an easy task. Nobody dared speak up to the devil, and certainly not to his wife!

Believe it or not, it was the *guanajos*, the turkeys, who suggested a solution. The *guanajos* were the devil's closest neighbors. They were the ones that suffered most from the fights, but they were also the ones who had the most fun when the devils were having a good day! *La Diabla* was a great cook and made delicious tamales. The devil, who was a great dancer, set the little devil to playing the *claves*, a little drum. And he would dance so beautifully! The devil would dance and jump so high that he could be seen from the *guanajos'* house. This is just what gave them their idea of how to get rid of the devil and his family.

The *guanajos'* proposal was very blunt. The animals would do the *baile sin cabeza*, the headless dance, as a pretext for cutting off the heads of the devil, *La Diabla*, and *El Diablito*.

The animals asked how this could be done. So the *guanajos* showed them how they could stick their head under their wing without actually losing it. In this way they would simulate a headless dance. They knew how much the devils enjoyed dancing. They were sure the devils would agree to be beheaded in order to be in the dance too.

The idea was approved and the danced arranged. The monkeys played the drums. The birds sang the melody. But the dance troupe consisted of twelve pair of *guanajos* who danced rhythmically with their heads under their wings, so that they appeared to be headless.

At the devil's house that day, sparks were flying. The devils were fighting because *La Diabla* said that she had the sharpest teeth. And the devil said that no, he had the largest and sharpest teeth. They were making such a racket that the little devil decided to go for a walk to avoid being in the middle of his parents' flames. The devil, unable to convince his wife, left the house with a slam of the door, which set the house on fire, and went down the road muttering to himself.

The devil hadn't gone far when he heard the beating of the drums, the singing of the birds, and feet stomping out a rhythm which drew him to the dance.

At the door was a welcoming committee formed by the oldest *guanajo*, a toad, and a bull. When the devil arrived, he asked to be let in immediately.

"No," said the old *guanajo*. "This is the *baile sin cabeza*, the dance without a head. Only those with no heads can enter." The devil peered in and saw that, sure enough, none of the dancers had a head! "Sorry," said the old guanajo. "You must leave your head at the door, if you wish to enter."

The devil didn't think this was a good idea. But at that very moment the orchestra began to play louder, and the birds sang:

"No baila! No baila! El que tiene cabeza no baila."
"Cannot dance! Cannot dance! He who has a head cannot dance!"

Those dancing inside were dancing so well and with such delight that the devil decided to give it a try. He laid his head on the guillotine, and the bull cut it off in a single stroke while the toad noted in his notebook: "First head falls." Then the vultures carried away the body and the head far from the place, and the dancing continued.

Meanwhile up on the mountain at the devil's house, *La Diabla* had to put out the flames in her house. Then she took a bath in vinegar so that she could be very sour when her husband returned.

She waited for a long time, but he didn't return. Time passed, and *La Diabla* became more and more annoyed wondering where her husband had gone that he did not come home. Since the devil wasn't showing his fangs around the house, she got dressed and went after him.

She wandered from one place to another, then, turning a bend in the road, she heard:

"No baila! No baila! El que tiene cabeza no baila."
"Cannot dance! Cannot dance! He who has a head cannot dance!"

She understood everything at once. It was certain that her husband was in that dance. She knew well how much he enjoyed dancing. With a sure step, she walked toward the place from which the music came. When she arrived, the band was playing and the *guana-jos* were dancing to the music. She asked if her husband was in there.

"It's hard to tell," said the doorkeepers. "Why don't you go in and look for yourself?"

She wanted to walk right in, but the old *guanajo* reminded her that this was a *baile sin cabeza*. No one could enter who had a head. She was so annoyed with her husband that, without thinking twice, she put her head on the guillotine, and the bull chopped it off while the toad wrote in his notebook: "Second head falls." Then the crows took charge of making *La Diabla's* body and head disappear.

The little son of the devil had waited for a long time outside the house so that his parents could calm down. Now he had returned to sleep. But the house was empty, and there was no trace of his parents. He worried about that, because even though they burned the house down every day, they always came back to sleep there. So he went out looking for them.

The little devil, who had very good hearing, at once heard the sounds, which by now could be heard all over the mountain. Knowing how much his parents enjoyed dancing, he went straight to the dance.

He arrived and noticed with puzzlement that the dancers inside had no heads, yet they danced really well. He asked the doorman if he had seen his parents go in.

"I couldn't say," said the old *guanajo*. "Why don't you go in and look for them?"

The little devil was about to walk right in. But the doorkeeper stopped him.

"Haven't you heard what the song says?"

"No baila! No baila! El que tiene cabeza no baila."
"Cannot dance! Cannot dance! He who has a head cannot dance!"

"Yes, but I'm not going to dance," said the little devil. "I'm just going to look for my parents."

"It doesn't matter. This is *el baile sin cabeza*. You cannot go in with your head on."

The little devil looked again. He wanted to find his parents, but cutting off his head was definitely not in his plans. Inside, the band played even more loudly and the birds sang strongly:

"No baila! No baila! El que tiene cabeza no baila."
"Cannot dance! Cannot dance! He who has a head cannot dance!"

The doorkeeper urged him to go in. But the little devil taking the road back home, said:

"No se si estan ahí todavia,
Pero esta cabecita mia
No me quitan ni a jodía."

"I don't know if they are still there,
But this head of mine?
Nobody takes off!"

And so today and forever more, there is still a devil in the world.

TELLING THIS STORY

When I tell this story, I scrunch my shoulders up like a headless turkey and dance the part. You can, of course, still flap your turkey wings. Just make up a tune to sing as you dance. If chopping off the heads seems too gross, you can just have them "remove their heads and set them down." The crows can carry them off while they are dancing.

PLAY WITH THIS STORY

Dance the Tale. Tell the story a second time and let everyone get up and dance the headless dance with you.

Act it out. You need three devils, a gatekeeper to remove the heads, and the rest can be turkeys.

ABOUT THIS STORY

This is an Afro-Cuban folktale collected by Samuel Feijóo and retold by Elvia Pérez. It contains motifs G520 *Ogre deceived into self-injury* and K890 *Dupe tricked into killing himself*. Note that Cuban folktales combine elements from African lore and Catholic traditions.

THE HERONS

Story collected by Martha Esquenazi, version by Elvia Pérez. For a Spanish version of this story see From the Winds of Manguito, *pp. 82–85.*

This is the story of two white herons that one day met, fell in love, laid their eggs, and then flew off. The eggs hatched by themselves, and after some time the shells cracked.

As soon as the little herons peeped out of their shells, they began to wonder who their mother and father were, because in truth, everyone in the world has a mother and father.

They were trying to find an explanation when the littlest one said, "If we have parents, we can find them by singing our song:

> *"Tin ganga o,*
> *tin ganga o*
> *yo mama ganga reré*
> *yayangrosio*
> *serecusere mi yayangrosio"*

This sounded like a really good idea. They took off flying in search of their parents, who are the most beautiful thing that one has.

After a while, they saw on the horizon a big, white bird that seemed a lot like their idea they had of their mother. So they asked, "Señora, are you by any chance our mother?"

That bird was a dove. She was so moved by those little herons all alone in the world that, without giving it much thought, she answered, "Yes, I am your mother."

Those little herons were so happy! Finally they had found their mother.

They were about to go off with her, when the littlest one asked, "Señora, do you sing?"

"Of course I do," replied the dove. And she sang,

> *"Si ambere, si ambere,*
> *bembere sió sió,*
> *si ambere si ambere,*
> *tu matitisao,*
> *marenbe regua o ya o sió."*

"Oh, what a pity, señora. That's not our song," said the little heron. "Our song is

> *"Tin ganga o,*
> *tin ganga o,*
> *yo mama ganga reré,*

yayangrosio,
serecusere mi yayangrosio"

After this they kept on flying. They were flying for quite a while searching for their parents in the blue sky. After a while, they saw in front of them a black bird. It didn't match their idea of their father at all. But when one searches for one's father one overlooks small details like colors. Without thinking, they shouted, "Señor, are you by any chance our father?"

This bird coming was the *totí*. It was not for nothing that this bird had a very bad reputation among the birds. He had always been jumping from party to party and from one girlfriend to the other. The *totí* was taken by surprise by those little herons that pretended to be his babies. He said to himself that he already had such a bad reputation, he didn't want to make it even worse. He didn't remember having babies, but if they said so . . . it was probably true! So he answered, "Yes, of course, I am your father."

Those little herons were so happy! Finally they had a father. They had all decided to go off with him, but the littlest one, who wasn't too sure, asked, "Señor, do you sing?"

Everybody knows that the *totí* doesn't sing or eat fruit, but since he already was in a tricky situation he didn't have a choice and had to answer, "Of course I sing! See? I sing:

"Rin cun cun tincu,
rin cun tin cun tin."

After trying to sing a couple more times, he decided to keep silent. That's when the little herons said, "What a pity, sir! You are not our father because our father would sing like this:

"Tin ganga o,
tin ganga o,
yo mama ganga reré,
yayangrosio,
serecusere mi yayangrosio"

After this, they kept going on their way. As they realized that they were not going to find their parents in the sky, they decided to look down on earth. They flew lower and started to look everywhere.

After a while they saw a woman who was doing her laundry under the heat of the noon sun. Her looks didn't resemble the idea that they had of their mother, but we know what happens when one looks for a mother, you overlook little details. They started to approach the woman carefully, because they could tell that the woman was in a very bad mood. Once they were within hearing distance, they asked, "Señora, could it be that you are our mother?"

The woman was very upset, not only because she had a huge pile of laundry to take care of, but also because the sun was terribly hot. She thought that the little herons were making fun of her with their question. Without looking at them she snapped, "Yeah, *sure.* I'm your mother."

The little birds noticed that the woman had very bad manners, but when it comes to one's own mother, everything is forgiven. They were trying to get a little closer to help her out with the laundry when the littlest one asked, "Señora, do you sing?"

The woman thought, "How dare they ask me to sing, with all the work I have to do." Gritting her teeth, she snarled, "Sure. I sing.

"Sopua sopua! Just see me wash!"

The little herons started to move away from that furious woman, and when they were far enough away to be safe, they said, "What a pity, señora! You are not our mother either, because our mother would sing,

"Tin ganga o,
tin ganga o,
yo mama ganga reré,
yayangrosio,
serecusere mi yayangrosio"

The little herons kept going their way, but even though they had looked around the sky and around the earth, they hadn't found their father or their mother. They were very tired and decided to go down to a pond to drink. There they were when they saw a strange creature stumbling along. It didn't look like their idea of their mother. But when one is searching for a mother, one doesn't get stopped by little things. They opened their beaks and said, "Señora, is it possible that you may be our mother?"

The creature coming along was a turtle! She had been all night at a party drinking cane liquor and was so drunk that she didn't care if she was someone's mother or not. When between the fogginess of the hangover she got a glimpse of the little herons, she thought that they were very funny. She replied, "Of course! That's exactly who I am!"

How happy those little herons were! Of course, their mother was in such bad shape that she needed to be bathed and taken to bed, but what is there that one won't do for one's own parent? They were about to start fulfilling what they considered their duty, when the littlest one that wasn't so sure about the turtle asked, "Señora, do you sing?"

This turtle was full of fun. There wasn't a birthday party or *guateque* that she didn't attend. So she replied, "I sing, I dance, and I play the kettledrum! See? I just finish composing a *son* that goes,

"Poor Don Pedro
musenlá musenlá,
poor Don Pedro
musenlá musenlá,
I am going home,
musenlá musenlá."

As she said this, she fell into the pond and left the little herons as they were before, without a father or a mother. They decided to return to their nest and wait for their parents there. They drank some water and were about to leave when they saw two large white birds coming. They very much looked like the idea they had of their father and mother. So they took courage and asked, "Señora, señor, could it be that you are our parents?"

And of course these were the same white herons that one day fell in love, laid their eggs, and flew away, and that were now returning to their nest. They were very proud of their beautiful babies. They answered, "Yes, we are your parents!"

They were so happy! Finally they had a father and a mother, which is the most wonderful thing one has in life. They were about to go off with these parents, when the littlest one, that was still suspicious, asked, "But, do you sing?"

And the big herons sang:

> "Tin ganga o,
> tin ganga o,
> yo mama ganga reré. . . ."

They couldn't finish their song, because the little herons flew towards them and started to kiss them with their beaks and hug them with their wings. The turtle, who after a cold bath swam back to the surface, tells us that when they flew off into the blue, blue sky, for a long, long time one could hear the song echoing from the mountains:

> "Tin ganga o,
> tin ganga o,
> yo mama ganga reré,
> yayangrosio,
> serecusere mi yayangrosio"

TELLING THIS STORY

Create a sweet tune to use when singing the Mother Bird's "Tin ganga o. . . ." If the Cuban rhyme is too difficult, just sing, "Tin ganga o. . . tin ganga o. . . . I am your mother. Tin ganga o. . . ." The chants are not in Spanish, but in an Afro-Cuban dialect.

PLAY WITH THIS STORY

Act it out. It is fun to act this story out. Assign parts, station the mother birds and turtle around the room, then lead the rest of the children as baby birds in a search for their mother.

Read a picture book variant. This story is very much like the Mende folktale "Kanji-Jo, the Nestlings" in Margaret Read MacDonald's *Tuck-Me-In Tales* (August House, 1996). Read this story aloud and show the pictures. Encourage the children to sing along with you on the baby bird's chants.

ABOUT THIS STORY

This is a variant of the Mende folktale "Kanji-Jo, the Nestlings" in Margaret Read MacDonald's *Tuck-Me-In Tales* (Little Rock: August House, 1996). She found versions of the tale from four different Mende tellers. It is related in some ways to Z32.3.2.1 *Mouse seeks singing husband.* In which a mouse asks suitors to sing so she can choose the best spouse.

ABOUT THE STORYTELLER

ELVIA PÉREZ heard stories from her grandparents in a tiny *batey* (neighborhood) called Manguito, located near the town of San Antonio de las Vueltas, in Villa Clara province, in the central area of the island of Cuba. She lived there until she was four, and after that her family returned from the city to Manguito for every holiday. She writes: "The thing I owe most to San Antonio de las Vueltas is the marvelous stories told by my grandmother Luz, or by my father, by my cousin Susana, by my uncles and cousins, and so many persons of the countryside, who used fantastic stories and humorous tales to fill the nights when our family got together. Or to lighten the days of work in the fields."

Elvia now travels throughout North and South America telling her Cuban tales at festivals and performances. She organizes a biannual storytelling festival in Habana.

ABOUT THE TRANSLATOR AND EDITOR

Argentinian teller Paula Martín met Elvia when she and Margaret Read MacDonald were telling stories at a festival in Habana organized by Elvia. Paula is also author of *Pachamama*, see pp. 149–155. Margaret has twice visited Cuba as part of Elvia's storytelling festivals.

FINLAND

From *The Enchanted Wood and Other Tales from Finland* by Norma J. Livo and George O. Livo (Libraries Unlimited, 1999).

HOW THE TREES LOST THEIR POWER OF SPEECH

Back in the old days, when everything was peaceful, a man went into the forest to cut some firewood. He came up to a likely-looking birch tree and got ready to cut it down. Just as he was ready to swing his axe, the birch begged plaintively, "Allow me to live! I am still a young tree and have many children who need me and would mourn my death."

Never before had a tree spoken to the woodcutter. He took pity on the birch tree and went on to an oak tree. Again he was just ready to swing his axe when the oak stopped him in mid-swing. "Let me live! I am still strong and robust. My acorns are unripe and unfit for planting. Where will future generations get oak wood if I and my acorns are to be destroyed?"

Again, the man listened to this argument, so he moved over to an ash tree, which wailed, "Let me live! I am young. I got married only yesterday. What will become of my wife, poor thing, if you kill me now?"

The woodcutter went over to a maple tree, and it too begged, "Let me live! My sap is now flowing, and I have to feed many small creatures with it. What will become of them if you cut me down?"

And so it went with every tree. Each begged the woodcutter for mercy in a human voice. Never could the woodcutter cut these trees down. The aspen tree asked for mercy because, "I was created to rustle my leaves in the wind and to frighten the wrongdoers from their wicked ways."

"I have to give shelter to the singing birds, and the birds would leave the country if I get cut down. The people would be deprived of the beautiful singing of the birds!" said the wild cherry tree.

Even the mountain ash had a reason for why it should not be cut down: "The clusters of my berries are still growing. In order to provide the birds with food during the fall and winter, my berries are needed. What would become of the poor birds if I were hacked down right now?"

"Well," thought the man, "I guess I will chop down the fir trees."

But the spruce and the pine he went to next also begged him to spare them, saying, "We have to stay green to adorn nature, especially in winter."

The juniper, of whom it is said that it is the real treasure of the woods and the bringer of happiness to all creatures, animals as well as men, begged especially hard to be spared. "My juice cures ninety-nine diseases. Why would you want to kill me?"

What could the poor compassionate woodcutter do but pass the juniper by? He sat on a hillside in deep meditation. "What will I do now? How dare I go home empty-handed? My wife is waiting for wood to use in the stove for cooking and heating."

As he sat there, troubled, an old man with a long gray beard stepped out of the forest. He wore a shirt of birch bark and a coat of spruce bark. The newcomer walked over to the woodcutter and asked him, "What is troubling you?"

The woodcutter told him his story about how he had found the trees alive and full of their own wishes and their own language. He also told the old man that he couldn't resist their arguments for mercy. The stranger gave him a cheerful look and thanked him for having spared his children and for listening to their requests. As a token of his gratitude, he gave the woodcutter a rod of gold that would fulfill all of his wishes in the future. He also warned the cutter to take care that the wishes should never be extravagant or impossible, or else misfortune would happen instead of happiness.

If the woodcutter wanted to build a building, he had only to go to an anthill, wave the rod three times over it, and explain how the work was to be done. By next morning his orders would be followed. If he needed food, he had only to tell the kettle what he wanted. If he wanted some sweets, he had to show the rod of gold to the bees, and they would bring him more honeycomb than he and his family would ever be able to use.

The trees would give him sap, milk, and healing juice. If he needed silk, linen, or woolen fabrics, spiders would weave just as he desired them.

"I am the spirit of the woods," said the stranger. "I have been assigned to rule over the trees." After he said that, he disappeared.

Back home, the woodcutter's wicked wife met him angrily and insulted him when she saw him returning without the wood. "All the birch twigs should gather into bunches of rods and whip those who are lazy," she told him.

"Let it happen just as you wish," said the woodcutter, waving the rod, and the quarrelsome wife got a good spanking! He was quite pleased when he saw that his golden rod had become a corrector of his bad-tempered wife.

Next, the woodcutter decided to try out the building ability of the ants. He ordered them to build him a new grain storehouse in the backyard. The very next morning it was finished. There was no one happier than the woodcutter. The kettle cooked and served his food. Spiders wove wonderful fabrics. The moles plowed his fields. Ants sowed seeds in the spring and gathered his crops in the fall. He didn't need the help of a human hand anymore.

The woodcutter lived happily to the end of his life. He was careful to heed the warning of the wood spirit and never wished for impossible things, nor was he greedy. At his death, he left the magic rod to his children. It was also a great blessing for them.

Years later, in the third generation, the rod became the property of a foolish man who disobeyed the orders of his parents and began to demand all kinds of absurd things. He wanted to test the power of the rod, so one day he ordered it to bring the sun down from the heaven to warm his back. As it was impossible to fulfill this wish, hot rays shot down from the sun. They burned up the offender, his house, and all of his belongings. No trace was left of the place where the foolish man had lived. This was the punishment for his disobedience.

The magic rod was probably melted in the fire, for nobody ever found it. It is believed that the trees in the woods became so frightened by the fire that they lost their power of speech forever. Nobody since that time has heard a word from trees, but they do whisper and whisper among themselves.

PLAY WITH THIS STORY

Act it out. This is a wonderful story to act out. Many teachers have turned it into a class play to share the value of trees with their students. You can change the types of trees to reflect the trees in your local forests, add more trees, and adapt it to fit your needs.

ABOUT THIS STORY

Several folktale motifs refer to prohibitions about cutting down trees: Motif C518 *Cutting down tree tabu*; C51.2.2 *Tabu: cutting sacred trees or groves*; and D1610.2 *Speaking tree*. For an Estonian version of this tale, see *The Sea Wedding and Other Stories from Estonia* by Selve Maas and Peggy Hoffman (Minneapolis: Dillon Press, 1970). For another fun-to-tell version, see "Mikku and the Trees" in *Earth Care: World Folktales to Talk About* by Margaret Read MacDonald (Atlanta: August House, 2005), pp. 22–27.

THE CAT AND MOUSE

Ages ago there was a cat and a mouse who were friends. "Let's gather our winter supplies," suggested the cat. The cat, being wealthier and quicker of wit, got an earthen pot. The mouse began to store up fat in the pot.

Soon the pot was filled. A dog, however, had smelled the fat in the air and began to sniff around for the fat pot.

The mouse said to the cat, "My friend, our fat pot is in danger. We must take it to a safer place."

"Very good, my friend. The dog is after it and getting closer," replied the cat. They carried the fat pot to the church and hid it in the basement under the altar. The following Sunday the cat said, "Today I have been asked to stand sponsor at a christening, and so I must go to church."

"Go if you must, but do not forget to have a look at our fat pot," advised the mouse. Later in the evening the mouse asked the name of the cat's godchild.

"A Little Off," was the answer.

"That is a peculiar name. Never in my life have I heard anything like that," squeaked the mouse.

The following Sunday the cat went again to the church to stand sponsor at another christening. "What name was given to this godchild?" questioned the mouse when the cat returned from church.

"Half Gone," the cat replied.

On the third Sunday the same thing happened. This time the godchild's name was "Some Left." On the fourth Sunday it was "Bottom Bare."

"Aha, friend, now I know what you meant by those names," cried the mouse. "The first time you ate a little of the fat, then a half, then some was still left, and at last all the fat was gone. You emptied our fat pot, old friend! You are a deceiver and a thief!"

"How dare you insult me," screamed the cat. "You wretched creature!" In an instant the cat caught the mouse and ate it without pity. From that time on, no mouse has ever sought the friendship of a cat.

PLAY WITH THIS STORY

Tell and erase. Draw a pot on the white board and color it yellow. Let one child tell each episode of the story and erase the yellow "butter" from a portion of the pot.

Demonstrate one-fourth, half, and three-fourths. Draw four pots. Color the first one-fourth full, the second half full, the third three-fourths full, and the fourth completely full.

ABOUT THIS STORY

This is motif K372 *Playing godfather.* Type 15. It appears in Grimm's fairy tales, and MacDonald cites African American variants as well as some from Scotland, France, Russia, and Puerto Rico.

ABOUT THE AUTHORS

NORMA J. LIVO is a retired professor of education at the University of Colorado, Denver. She is former board member of the National Storytelling Association and recipient of the National Storytelling Association's Leadership Award and the 1995 Colorado Governor's Award for Excellence in the Arts. She is author of many award-winning books on storytelling.

GEORGE O. I. LIVO, a geologist with a career in worldwide oil and mineral exploration, was born in Finland. He contributed his considerable knowledge of Finnish lore to the collection.

GREECE

From *Folktales from Greece: A Treasury of Delights*. Retold by Soula Mitakidou and Anthony L. Manna, with Melpomeni Kanatsouli (Libraries Unlimited, 2002).

KALLO AND THE GOBLINS

Once, in Greece, there was a mother who had two daughters, Marbo and Kallo. Kallo, the youngest, was as beautiful as Marbo, the oldest, was ugly.

As they were growing up, Marbo became more and more jealous of her sister. And why not? Wherever they went, people admired Kallo and praised her beauty and kindness, but they only felt pity for Marbo.

Soon, Marbo felt no desire to leave the house. Every time her mother urged her to go out, Marbo would refuse and tell her to send Kallo. And Kallo, always eager to please, would do all the chores.

One day, on Christmas Eve, as their mother was getting ready to make the traditional Christmas sweets, she looked inside the pantry and could find no flour.

"Marbo, will you go to the mill and grind some wheat?" the mother asked.

"No," Marbo replied. "Send Kallo."

Willingly, Kallo loaded their little donkey with two sacks of wheat and went to the mill.

When Kallo reached the mill, she was surprised to find so many people waiting their turn to grind their wheat. By the time Kallo's turn came, the sun had set and it had grown dark. The miller poured her wheat onto the millstone and went to his room to sleep. Left alone, Kallo sat on a pile of sacks and waited. It was dark in the mill with no other light but a small oil lamp.

Near midnight, Kallo heard footsteps. She turned toward the noise, and what did she see? A gang of hideous goblins was sneaking into the mill and coming toward her. You see, it was the Dodekameron, the Twelve Days of Christmas, when goblins come up to the earth to do their mischief.

The goblins gathered around Kallo and reached out to touch her with their long hands and sharp nails. Kallo remained still, frozen with terror.

"We'll eat you up, Kallo. We'll eat you up!" the goblins shrieked.

Despite her panic, Kallo was quick to say, "I know you are going to eat me, but you can't eat Kallo like this."

"How can we eat her then?" the goblins asked, curiously.

"Not in this old dress, you can't. Kallo needs a new dress," she replied.

"Dress?" the goblins wondered. "Quickly, let's go to bring her a dress." And off the goblins went in all directions.

"Dress . . . dress," they mumbled as they went here and as they went there. "Dress . . . dress . . . dress." They tried everything until they managed to sneak into a shop, choose the prettiest dress, and bring it to Kallo.

Again they surrounded the girl and cried, "We'll eat you up, Kallo. We'll eat you up."

"You can't eat Kallo like this," she replied. "You can't eat me barefooted on Christmas Eve! Kallo wants shoes."

"Shoes . . . shoes . . . shoes," echoed the goblins as they went off to bring her shoes.

They went here, and they went there. They did this, and they did that, until they brought Kallo the prettiest shoes.

"Now we'll eat you, Kallo!" they yelled.

"Oh, no, they do not eat Kallo like this. Kallo needs a coat too," she said.

"Coat . . . coat . . . coat," went the goblins as they set out again.

When they brought her that coat, Kallo asked for another, for a fur coat. And when they brought her the fur coat, she asked for an umbrella. And then gloves. And then a comb. And then face powder. And . . . name it, she asked for it.

So, with this and that, the new day dawned. When the roosters crowed, the goblins rushed to hide in their holes, for goblins can't live in daylight.

Soon the miller woke up, ground the wheat, and loaded the flour on Kallo's donkey. In the meantime, Kallo tied all the things the goblins had given her onto the saddle. Then she started back to her village.

Now, her mother had been very worried about Kallo, but when she saw her returning with all those things, her worry turned to surprise.

"What's all this?" both her mother and sister asked.

"Things the goblins gave me at the mill," Kallo answered.

Marbo said nothing but put it in her mind to go to the mill and ask the goblins to bring her gifts too. She had to hurry, though. There was very little time until Epiphany, the day when priests go out with holy water to banish goblins and other evil spirits.

So Marbo took all the flour from the pantry and spilled it here and there. By New Year's Eve it was all gone.

"We have no flour again," the mother said. "Which one of you will go to the mill and grind some wheat?"

"This time, I'll go!" Marbo cried.

She loaded the donkey with wheat and set off. But she took her time to make sure she would have to spend the night at the mill. It was dark when she arrived.

At around midnight, the goblins appeared. Immediately they charged at Marbo.

"We'll eat you up, Marbo. We'll eat you up!" they cried.

"Help!" Marbo screamed. "Goblins are eating me."

The miller heard her and ran to her rescue. But, by the time he lit his torch, the goblins had reached the girl and scratched her face.

Marbo returned to her village even uglier than before.

Seeing her sister so sad and unhappy, Kallo took pity on her and gave her half of the goblins' gifts. And the goblins' face powder? It worked miracles, and Marbo's wounds were soon healed.

And so the two sisters and their mother lived well for the rest of their days.

But we lived better.

PLAY WITH THIS STORY

Dress a paper doll. Make a photocopied paper doll of a girl and her accessories—dress, shoes, coat, gloves, umbrella—for the children tell the story with.

Share other Kind and Unkind Girl stories.

Papa Gatto: An Italian Fairy Tale by Ruth Sanderson (Boston: Little, Brown, 1990).

Mufaro's Beautiful Daughters: An African Tale by John Steptoe (New York: Lothrop, Lee & Shepard, 1987).

The Month Brothers: A Slavic Tale by Samuel Marshak, illustrated by Diane Stanley (New York: Morrow, 1983).

ABOUT THIS STORY

Q2.1 *Kind and unkind girls.* Type 480. *The Spinning-Woman by the Spring. The Kind and the Unkind Girls.* This story appears in many variants throughout the world. MacDonald's *Storyteller's Sourcebook* gives sources from France, England, Norway, Italy, Switzerland, Sri Lanka, Ireland, Appalachia, India, South Africa (Xhosa), West Africa, Japan, Haiti, Poland, Estonia, Greece, Bulgaria, Czechoslovakia, Latvia, Sweden, Denmark, Portugal, Venezuela, and Burma. Macdonald and Sturm cite African American versions as well as variants from France, Italy, Chile, Africa, Germany, England, Russia, India (Tamilnadu), Benin (Fon), Slovakia, and Siberia. A tale from Estonia in Diane Goode's *Diane Goode's Book of Scary Stories and Songs* (New York: Dutton, 1994), pp. 54–61, is very similar to this Greek tale, except that a mouse advises the girl to ask for the clothing.

A Note from the Authors

We based our version of "Kallo and the Goblins" on several sources: Fani Papalouka, *Istories San Paramythia* (Athens: Astir, 1960); "Ploumbo and Malamo," two versions found in Nikolaos Politis, *Paradoseia* (Athens: Ekdoseis Istoriki Erevna, 1904); and Haris Sakellariou, *Efthima Ellinika Laika Paramythia* (Athens: Kedros, 1987). Sakellariou collected this tale from a storyteller in the village of Agrapidia, in the south of Greece. For the sake of readers outside of Greece, we felt obliged to describe in the narrative certain Greek beliefs associated with religious and secular rituals.

According to Greek tradition, the *kallikantzari* are goblins who leave their underground homes each year, enter people's houses, and make their annual round of mischief during the Dodekameron, the Twelve Days of Christmas. These annoying creatures may be ancestors of spirits of the dead that ancient Greeks believed were released from Hades for a brief time each year to roam the earth and pester people. Ancient Greeks repelled these creatures by surrounding their temples with red thread or smearing their front doors with tar.

Some people imagine that the *kallikantzari* look human except for their remarkable height and astounding ugliness. Others see them as grotesque creatures with monkey arms, cleft hooves, and bodies covered with hair. Their main goal in life is to destroy the earth by chopping away at the tree that is believed to support it. When the tree is almost cut down, it is Christmastime, and according to their habit, they have to come up to the earth and pester people. The *kallikantzari* return to the underworld on the day of the Epiphany, January 6, when priests in the Greek Orthodox Church bless the waters with a crucifix.

ABOUT THE AUTHORS

SOULA MITAKIDOU is an education professor at Aristotle University of Thessaloniki.

ANTHONY L. MANNA teaches children's literature and drama at Kent State University.

They were assisted by Melpomeni Kanatsouli, children's literature professor at the University of Athens. Mitakidou and Manna are coauthors of the picture book *Mr. Semolina-Semolinus: A Greek Folktale*, illustrated by Giselle Potter (New York: Aladdin, 2004).

GUATEMALA

From *Mayan Folktales: Cuentos folklóricos mayas*. Retold and edited by Susan Conklin Thompson, Keith Steven Thompson, and Lidia López de López (Libraries Unlimited, 2007).

THE DWARF

"The Dwarf" is a tale about unseen inhabitants of an area with whom the locals are familiar but newcomers may have problems. Macario Chigüil, who lives in La Guitarra, Retalhuleu, Guatemala, told this story.

In the Department of Retalhuleu, in southwest Guatemala, there is a little hamlet called La Guitarra. On the plains around La Guitarra are cattle and horse ranches. It was to one of these ranches that many Mayan families emigrated from the cold highlands. Macario and his family were among those who moved there to work.

Macario's family consisted of two girls, two boys, and his wife. On the ranch they had a place to live, and the work Macario was going to do was to care for the cattle and the horses. The family settled themselves and looked for a school where the children could study. The oldest daughter was named Eleodora, but was affectionately called Lolita. The children had lots of room to play and enjoy themselves and pick the fruits that were produced in the area. Time passed, and Don Macario cared for the cows and the horses and planted crops.

One day Don Macario put away his horse, Pajarero, whom he always rode when he worked, then went to his house to rest. The next morning he got out his horse Pajarero, like every day, to ride to work. When he went to mount, he was surprised to see that his horse's tail was finely braided. He tried to unbraid the horse's tail. But that took more time and patience than he had, and he was not successful.

After a while he took Pajarero back to the stable again. He left and told the workers about the braid, and one of them told Don Macario that he had never heard of or seen anything like that happen to anyone on the farm.

Don Macario decided again to try to unbraid his horse Pajarero's tail. This time it was difficult, but he was patient enough to unbraid it. He told his friends and family that he was finally able to unbraid his horse's tail.

A week passed, and one morning upon arising very early, how surprised was Don Macario when he saw that the very long hair of his little girl Lolita was braided in the same way that Pajarero's tail had been. Lolita did not even know. Her father asked her if she had braided her hair the night before, and she answered no, that she had not, and that she always left her hair loose. They tried to unbraid Lolita's hair but could not do it. Then Don Macario, because he was very worried, went to look for the oldest man of La Guitarra hamlet to consult him about the situation that was occurring with his daughter's and his horse's hair.

The old man listened to him until the end and afterward broke into laughter. The old man said to him, "Ay, Macario, Macario, because you come from a faraway land you do not know the things that happen here. Those of us who work with the animals on the ranches know about the existence of the *nu'y* [pronounced new-ee], or dwarf, who loves to entertain himself by braiding the horses' tails during the night. And he does not like it at all if the braids are taken out like you did with the horse, so he braided Lolita's hair. Now what you must do is wait for the *nu'y*. As long as the *nu'y* returns to braid the tail of your horse he will be happy, and later you can unbraid the hair of your daughter Lolita."

Macario and his family did everything the old man had said to them. The *nu'y* came back and braided the tail of the horse Pajarero, and so they were able to unbraid Lolita's hair and everything returned to normal. They continued to live happily in La Guitarra, with the knowledge of secret things.

PLAY WITH THIS STORY

Braid ribbons. Provide colorful ribbons (paper or cloth) and help children learn to braid. Tie the ribbon to a chair back or table leg so it can be pulled tight as you braid.

ABOUT THIS STORY

Tales of horses' manes and tails braided by elves are common throughout Latin America. The motif of the daughter's hair being braided is more unusual. Stith Thompson cites a German tale: F451.5.1.13 *Dwarf washes, combs, and braids hair for sleeping maids.*

ABOUT THE STORYTELLER

MACARIO CHIGÜIL lives in La Guitarra hamlet, Retalhuleu, Guatemala. He likes to tell this story to his four sons. He says the story is special to him because it is based on his own experience and because it emphasizes coexistence with animals. Horses are important in the life of La Guitarra.

ABOUT THE AUTHOR

Susan Conklin Thompson is a professor in the education department at the University of Northern Colorado. She travels frequently to Guatemala with her husband, Keith Thompson, who is a hydrologist. Lidia López de López of San Antonio Aguas Calientes, Guatemala, assisted them with collecting, translating, and preparing the tales in their book.

HAITI

From *When Night Falls, Kric! Crac! Haitian Folktales* by Liliane Nérette Louis. Edited by Fred Hay (Libraries Unlimited, 1999).

BOUKI WINS THE KING'S CONTEST
The Contest for Princess Moon

The King had a daughter who was very beautiful, so beautiful that when she was born, the King did not know what to name her. Finally, he called his daughter Moon. Moon in the Sky, for she was that lovely. Her skin was black and beautiful, and she had long, black hair.

Moon was a kind princess, the joy of everyone in the kingdom. Every morning the King would parade with his daughter. Young men would come and offer flowers to Moon, and she would accept them graciously, with a smile.

When Moon grew up, her father, the King, did not know who should be the lucky man to marry her. None of the eligible men were acceptable.

One day the King said, "I know what I will do. I shall have a contest, because I want the most intelligent man of this kingdom to marry my daughter."

The next day the King sent his guards all over town, announcing the contest with trumpets and drums. All the men in town were happy to hear the news. Even Bouki was excited, thinking he could marry Princess Moon.

Bouki ran over to Malis's home. "Malis! Malis! Did you hear the news? The King is having a contest. Whoever wins the contest will marry Princess Moon."

Malis laughed at the excitement of Bouki. "So what, "Bouki? What does this have to do with you?"

"I can marry Moon," said Bouki. "In the palace there is lots of food, and I can eat meat all day. Malis, do you think you need a Bouki like me to tell you that?"

"Mennen koulév leko pa difsil se fé l'chita ki red (Leading a snake to school is not hard, but making him sit is the trouble)," said Malis.

"You will see," answered Bouki.

The next day, early morning, all the young men lined up in front of the palace. The long line extended past the school and the church. Every man in line was eager to become the husband of Moon, the most beautiful princess a kingdom had ever seen.

The King came out on the balcony, and the crowd applauded.

Bouki was in line, but everyone kept pushing him back. "Get out of here, Bouki. You are too stupid! You can't marry that beautiful princess."

The King said, "I repeat. Anyone can marry Moon, if he can win the contest to prove his intelligence. I want a very intelligent man to marry my daughter. The contest will decide who shall be her husband.

"I will throw an orange into the air. The man who can count to ten before the orange reaches my hand shall marry my beautiful daughter, Princess Moon."

Every man in the crowd responded with a *houha, houha, houha.* They were all laughing, pushing Bouki to the back of the line.

Then the contest began. The first man approached. The King tossed an orange into the air, and the man said, "1-2-3-4-5-6-7-8-9-10." But the orange was in the King's hand before the man counted six.

The next man came forward. He counted very fast, but not fast enough. The next man was the same. And the next, and the next, and the next.

All day people heard, "Get back, Bouki. You've never been to school. You don't know how to count." And all day people heard "1-2-3-4-5-6-7-8-9-10." Again and again, the King threw the orange into the air, and again and again young men tried to count faster than the orange fell. Again and again they pushed Bouki to the back of the line.

It was getting very late, and no one had won the contest. Finally, it was Bouki's turn. The King said, "Give Bouki his chance. My kingdom is one of justice. Bouki may try, just like everyone else."

Bouki looked at the King, and Bouki looked at the orange. It was true: Bouki did not know how to count. As the king tossed the orange into the air, Bouki said, "One, ten!" That was what Bouki had heard all day long: "One, ten!" as the men counted so fast. So that is what he said, "One, ten!"

His majesty the King said, "Did I hear ten? Did I hear ten? Did I hear ten? Yes, I heard ten! Bouki wins the contest! Bouki shall marry Princess Moon."

Bouki was happy. Bouki started to dance. Bouki started to sing. Bouki said over and over, "From now on, I can eat meat all day and night!"

The Disastrous Marriage

The next day the village was filled with festivity, because Bouki was marrying Princess Moon. At the reception, Bouki ate and ate. It was embarrassing. Bouki ate lots of meat: *griyo* (pork), chicken, barbecued goat, and beef. All that Bouki said to his beautiful wife was that he loved meat and he expected her to give him lots of meat.

The next morning when Bouki woke up, first thing he said to the princess was, "Where is my breakfast?"

When the servants took Bouki to the breakfast balcony, he looked at the food and said, "I don't want *akasan* (a popular Haitian cornmeal porridge sweetened with sugar cane syrup)." Bouki looked at the omelet they had made for him and said, "That's no food for Bouki. Bouki marry a princess. Bouki is living in a palace. Bouki must have meat, lots of meat, lots of meat."

The princess was disappointed. She went to the King. "Daddy, Daddy, that Bouki is not intelligent. He is stupid! He wants food all the time."

"My darling daughter Moon," said the King, "Bouki is your husband. You must do as he wants. Order the servants to kill cows, pigs, and chickens, and feed your husband as he pleases."

So the servants killed cows, pigs, and chickens. When Bouki came for supper, he said, "Now I see that I am married to a princess and I live in a palace. Bouki wants to eat like this every day."

From then on, at each meal there were three tables full of food! Bouki ate well, very well. After one such meal, the King said, "Let's go hunting."

And so the King, Bouki, and Princess Moon went hunting. The King took his *fizi* (gun).

In the forest, there were many wild birds. The King fired his gun: *dar dar dar dar dar.* He shot at once two wild chickens and three wild turkeys. Bouki jumped here; he jumped there. He gathered all the birds. He stuck some in his belt and some on his shoulder.

The King shot again: *dar dar dar dar dar.* More birds fell! Bouki was jumping and jumping and jumping here and there to gather the birds as they fell. He stuck some more in his belt and some more on his shoulders. He even stuck one on his head! Before you know it, Bouki was covered with feathers.

Bouki was so covered with feathers he looked like a big wild bird himself. Once again the King shot *dar dar dar dar dar.* This time, it was Bouki who got shot.

I heard Bouki yelling. I went to see what was wrong. Moon and the King kicked me—and here I am to tell the story.

TELLING THIS STORY

You might want to just share the contest half of the story and stress the counting aspect. Liliane tells me that she sometimes elaborates the story, saying that the children carried the Bouki-bird home and were about to stuff him in the oven when he jumped up and they realized their mistake.

PLAY WITH THIS STORY

Toss oranges. Hand out tangerines and let the children toss them in the air. See how far they can count before they catch the tangerine. You could also do this with wadded-up orange tissue paper.

Count by twos or fives. In other versions of this story, the task is solved by a trickster who counts by fives: "5, 10." Or by twos: "2, 6, 8, 10." This can be an introductory discussion of different ways to count.

Counting by twos: *Two Ways to Count to Ten: A Liberian Folktale* by Ruby Dee, illustrated by Susan Meddaugh (New York: Henry Holt, 1988).

Counting by fives: The story appears as a riddle tale, "The New Prince," in George Shannon, *More Stories to Solve* (New York: Greenwillow, 2001), and in *Teaching with Story: Classroom Connections to Storytelling* by Margaret Read MacDonald, Jennifer MacDonald Whitman, and Nathaniel Forrest Whitman (Atlanta: August House, 2013).

ABOUT THIS STORY

This is Motif H331.18* *Suitor contest: suitor must count to ten before spear he hurls reaches ground. Small antelope counts five, ten, and wins.* The motif of counting by fives appears in other cultures too. A Welsh tale tells of a water-maiden who marries a human and is allowed to bring with her as many cattle as she can count in one breath. She counts by fives to get more. This story is found in Berlie Doherty, *Tales of Wonder and Magic* (Cambridge, MA: Candlewick, 1998), p. 18.

Bouki is a standard character in Haitian folktales. Liliane Nérette Louis's collection includes several other stories about Bouki. Another fun story about Bouki winning a contest from the King appears in *The Magic Orange Tree and Other Haitian Folktales* by Diane Wolkstein (New York: Shocken, 1997). In that lively singing story he wins a dance contest!

MOTHER FROG AND HER TWELVE CHILDREN

A long time ago, in Haiti, lived the Frog family: Mother Frog, Father Frog, and their 12 children frogs. Mother Frog was always very busy, because the children were lazy and refused to help with the chores around their house.

The children frogs were so lazy each one of them had adopted a tree to hide behind, so Mother Frog could not find them when she came looking for them.

Mother Frog was always thinking, "If I did not have so many children, maybe I could prepare the food more easily and I would not be so tired." But 12 frog children!

Mother Frog had to clean the house, go to the river to get water, carry the dry wood on her head, and gather all the insects for the day's meal. At night, when she complained to her husband, Father Frog, about all the work, he said, "I work in the field. I gave you 12 frogs to help you. It is no fault of mine if you are tired."

Mother Frog never gave up, but every day it was the same refrain.

Mother Frog, "Frog children, gather the wood for the fire."

Frog children, "No, we are not capable."

Mother Frog, "Frog children, take the bucket, go to the river for water."

Frog children, "No, we are not capable."

Mother Frog, "Frog children, take coffee to the field to your father."

Frog children, "No, we are not capable."

Mother Frog, "Frog children, give some help to your mother.

Frog Children, "No, we are not capable."

Mother Frog, "Any help, frog children?"

Frog children, "No, no, no, we are not capable."

Mother Frog had to prepare all the food by herself. Finally, when it was ready, Mother Frog said, "Let me go call on my children to eat."

Mother Frog, "Frog children, the food is ready."

Frog children, "For that we will try.

VAT-E VAT-E VAT-E-VAT
FOR THAT WE WILL TRY.

Mother Frog watched her 12 frog children hop out from behind their trees. They were all singing.

VAT-E VAT-E VAT-E-VAT
FOR THAT WE WILL TRY.

Mother Frog was sad. "I will never get any help from my children," she said. "I must do something about this deplorable situation." Then Mother Frog remembered a Haitian proverb:

Bourik fé pitit pou do'l poze.
Donkey has kids so his back can rest.

"But for me," Mother Frog said, "there is never any rest for me!"

A donkey passing by heard Mother Frog. He volunteered to help her. "You must be brave," the donkey said. "Tomorrow, when the food is ready, I will teach your children a lesson."

"Are you sure you can teach them a lesson, Donkey?" said Mother Frog. "If you do, I will pay you with a good portion of fresh herbs."

"I am sure I can teach them a lesson, but you don't need to pay me," said Donkey. "I will compensate myself."

The next day, when the frog children heard, "The food is ready," they immediately came from behind their trees. But this time donkey was there. With his "Hi-han, hi-han, hi-han," he gulped down all the food. Then he said,

"Who don't work, hi-han, hi-han.
Who don't eat, hi-han, hi-han."

Ever since that day, all 12 frogs have always helped their mother. And now, you never see a frog without seeing her offspring following her!

I went to look for the donkey, because I needed him to teach a lesson to my own boys. When I found the donkey, he gave me the biggest kick of my life—and here I am to tell the story.

PLAY WITH THIS STORY

Act it out. This is a fun story to act out. You need a strong speaker for Mother Frog. Everyone else can hide around the room and call out from behind their "trees," "No we aren't able!" Repeat this twice. The next day it is exactly the same thing. You can be Donkey and come eat everything up and admonish the frogs.

ABOUT THIS STORY

Note that many Haitian stories end with the storyteller being given a big kick—kicked all the way here to tell the story.

This is a similar to W111.6* *The Little Red Hen and the Grain of Wheat*. Find versions of that tale in *The Little Red Hen* by Byron Barton (New York: HarperCollins, 1993). And find versions of the traditional folktale in many collections, such as *Tomie de Paola's Favorite Nursery Tales* by Tomie de Paola (New York: Putnam, 1989).

For a Siberian version, see "Pancake Party" in *Three Minute Tales: Stories from Around the World to Tell or Read when Time Is Short* by Margaret Read MacDonald (Atlanta: August House, 2004), pp. 36–37. Raven and Snow Ptarmigan refuse to help Mouse make pancakes, but are eager to help eat them.

A Note from the Storyteller

Liliane Nérette Louis writes: When I was growing up, storytelling was a major source of entertainment in Haiti. When night fell, the whole family would gather around a central figure—usually the grandmother, sometimes the mother, sometimes a grandpa or an aunt or an older sister or brother, or a maid—to listen to stories.

But the stories were not just entertainment. In the Haitian home, as in the Haitians' African homeland, grownups use stories to educate, and especially to teach right and wrong. As a child, I experienced this. When I did something wrong during the day, my mother would wait until evening. Then, in a beautiful folktale, she would convey her message about my wrongdoing. No one would easily forget her beautiful stories—or her message of right and wrong.

At a very young age, these stories attracted me. Even though I am number four in a family of eight, I was the traditional sister who passed the stories on to the youngest. Later, I passed them on to my children, who loved to hear about Bouki's stupidities, even though all three of my children were born in New York City. Haitian folktales are a treasure of our culture. Now that they are becoming an endangered art form, I feel it is my duty to preserve them.

Once upon a time, I found myself in a classroom in Haiti teaching 58, ranging from 7 to 11 years of age. Many of the children had never been to school before; three-fourths of them could not recognize the first letter of the alphabet. But they had even greater difficulties to overcome. The children had no food to eat. They would come to school hungry and could not pay attention. So I would tell them stories. Those stories helped to make up for some of the things that were missing from their lives. My students were undeniably poor, but stories were something I could freely give and poverty could never take away.

ABOUT THE STORYTELLER AND EDITOR

LILIANE NÉRETTE LOUIS lives in Florida, where she has received many awards for her storytelling work, including a bronze medal from the Historical Association of Southern Florida.

Fred Hay is librarian of the W.L. Aury Appalachian Collection and a professor at the Center for Appalachian Studies, Appalachian State University in Boone, North Carolina. His publications include African American community studies and the ethnography and folklore of African Appalachia.

HMONG

From *Folk Stories of the Hmong: Peoples of Laos, Thailand, and Vietnam* by Norma J. Livo and Dia Cha (Libraries Unlimited, 1991).

THE ORPHAN AND THE MONKEYS

Thousands of years ago, there was an orphan who lived with his elder brother and sister-in-law. His sister-in-law did not like him. In fact, she planned to kill him. The orphan was very sad and cried because he was so lonely.

His sister-in-law gave him dried seeds to plant, and everyone knows that dried seeds are no good for growing things. But he sowed all of the seeds in the field. Of course, many of them did not grow, but surprisingly, some of the seeds did sprout.

As the plants in his garden grew and the grain ripened, the monkeys kept stealing his corn and rice. The orphan decided to ask the *shoa*, or wise man, for help.

"Why do the monkeys keep coming to take all of my corn?" the orphan asked the *shoa*. "I can't make them stay away. I am a poor man, and I need all the crops I can grow."

"Go home, kill a chicken, cook it, and eat some of it. Put some of what is left in your nose, your eyes, and your ears. Then go to the path made by the monkeys and go to sleep in the middle of it," counseled the wise man.

The orphan did as he was told. He killed a chicken, boiled it in water, and ate some of it. Afterwards he put some of the chicken in his eyes, his ears, and his nose. He found the monkeys' trail and lay down in the middle of it and went to sleep.

The monkeys found him on the trail and thought he was dead. "Who died here?" they asked. They picked up the orphan and carried him to the mountains where they lived. The monkeys had a big funeral ceremony for the dead farmer and invited many animals to come and join them. All the animals that came brought gold and money to put around the orphan as he lay on the blanket.

Suddenly the farmer sat up and lunged at the animals, yelling "Yah-h-h-h!" as loudly as he could. All of the shocked and frightened animals ran away. The monkeys ran up into the trees.

Then the orphan calmly picked up all the gold and silver and went home a rich man. When he got to the home of his brother and sister-in-law and showed them the fortune, they asked him, "Where did you get all of those riches?"

The Orphan and the Monkeys

He told them the story of the monkeys and how he had tricked them. And so, the orphan lived with his family and shared his wealth with them. He was never sad or lonely again.

PLAY WITH THIS STORY

Act it out. Place a blanket in the "path" for the orphan to lie on and pretend to be lifeless. The monkeys should have gold pieces to sprinkle around the lifeless orphan. Then they pick up the corners of the blanket and try to carry him off. He jumps up and scares them away. Repeat with a different orphan.

ABOUT THIS STORY

Macdonald cites a Japanese version of this tale, J2415.23* *Farmer disguised as scarecrow taken for Jizo statue by monkeys.* For a Chinese variant, see "The Big Man Drum: A Dai folktale from China" in *Shake-it-up Tales: Stories to Sing, Dance, Drum, and Act Out* by Margaret Read MacDonald (August House, 2000), pp. 75–80. In most versions of this story the brother (or another man) imitates the lucky man's actions and ends up with an unpleasant reward.

WHY BIRDS ARE NEVER HUNGRY

A long time ago, when the world was new, there were two brothers who went hunting. After the long day of walking through the jungle, they got lost. They were worried and could not remember which way to go to get back home to their parents. For many days, they wandered in the jungle. They did not have anything to eat and became very hungry.

One day the older brother decided that he had to go to find food and wood for the fire. The younger brother also wanted to go to gather water. After they discussed their plans, they each went their own way. They agreed to meet back at the clearing in the forest where they were camping when they had gathered the necessary things.

The younger brother went up and down everywhere through the jungle, but he could not find any water. Finally, he was so tired he sat down on a stone to think. He tried to face in a different direction, thinking he might find water that way. While he was thinking, a bluebird was jumping from one tree to another, singing, "I know where your parents are, I know where your parents are!"

The younger brother was surprised, because he wasn't sure what he was really hearing. He stared at the bluebird and tried to listen more carefully. He hoped the bluebird would sing to him and say those words again. He watched the bluebird wherever it went. After a time the bluebird started to sing again, saying the same words. The younger brother asked the bluebird, "Did you say you know where our parents are?"

"Yes, I did. But this is a bargain. If you can give me three insects then I will lead you to your parents," the bluebird chirped.

The boy paused a while and then he said, "Are you sure? If you are sure, will you also follow me now while I go to get my older brother?"

The bird agreed.

As the bargain had been set, the bluebird followed the younger boy to the clearing in the forest, where the older brother was sitting and waiting. He had been there for a long time and had returned without either the food or the wood. The younger brother told the older brother about his bargain with the bluebird. Then the brothers left the bird in the clearing and went to find the insects. It took them quite some time, but they finally returned to the clearing and gave the insects to the bluebird.

After the bluebird had eaten the insects, he said, "You boys must follow me wherever I fly and I will lead you to your parents."

The bluebird flew away, leading the two boys. They followed the bird closely, and after many days they finally got home. They were very happy, and they thanked the bluebird many times for leading them safely home.

PLAY WITH THIS STORY

Make a paper bluebird. Fold a piece of blue construction paper in half. Trace a bird shape with the bird's back on the fold. Cut out your bird. Attach a string to the middle of the bird's back. Run and watch the bird fly behind you.

Act out the story using your bluebirds. Work in pairs. One child is the lost boy, the other is the bluebird. The boy finds insects to feed the bluebird. Then the bluebird flies off to the boy's home and the boy follows. The "home" should be a designated space where all the children reassemble at the story's end.

ABOUT THIS STORY

This tale includes motifs B151.2 *Bird determines road to be taken* and B172 *Magic bird.*

ABOUT THE AUTHORS

NORMA J. LIVO was a professor of education at the University of Colorado at Denver. She is a well-known storyteller and author of *Bringing Out Their Best: Values Education and Character Development through Traditional Tales* (Libraries Unlimited, 2003); *Story Medicine: Multicultural Tales of Healing and Transformation* (Libraries Unlimited, 2001); and many more storytelling titles.

DIA CHA is a Hmong immigrant from Laos and anthropologist. She is a professor of anthropology and ethnic studies at St. Cloud State University in St. Cloud, Minnesota.

INDIA

From *Jasmine and Coconuts: South Indian Tales* by Cathy Spagnoli and Paramasivam Samanna (Libraries Unlimited, 1999).

YES, DEAR, DO

Long ago in South India, a girl named Priya grew up and married Hari, a kind merchant. The couple lived peacefully with Hari's mother, but although all three worked very hard, they never had much to eat. So one day Hari said sadly to Priya, "There is not enough work here, Priya. I must go far away to earn some gold. Take care of my mother. Treat her as your mother. Help each other. I will return as soon as I can."

Priya tried to stop him, but he had to leave. She wrapped lemon rice, mango pickle, and her love in a banana leaf for him. His mother blessed him and cried softly after he left.

The two women cleaned, cooked, and stitched as before, but now the mother always seemed sad. Priya wondered how to help, how to make her stop missing her son. One day, Priya had an idea. She would ask the mother questions, all of the time, to keep her mind busy. She started right away.

"Amma, shall I sweep the floor?" Priya asked.

The mother looked up and forgot her worries as she answered, "Yes, dear, do."

Priya swept and soon asked, "Amma, shall I make tea now?"

The mother again forgot her sadness as she replied, "Yes, dear, do."

Priya kept on questioning, and the mother soon had no time to worry because she was so busy making replies.

"Amma, shall I go to the market?"

"Yes, dear, do."

"Amma, shall I light the oil lamp?"

"Yes, dear, do."

Even, "Amma, shall I go to the bathroom"

"YES, dear, DO."

Question followed question, and year followed year. Hari still had not returned. One day his mother, who was now quite old, became ill. Priya nursed her gently, but the older woman grew weaker and weaker. One day she spoke softly to Priya. "My dear, I have lived a long and good life. It is time now for me to leave. Take care and wait for my son."

"No, you cannot die. You can't leave me alone," begged Priya.

"I must," said the mother. "You will be fine."

"No, I will be too lonely. You are my only friend. Who will answer my questions?"

"I know you only asked them to help me," said the mother. "And they did. Thank you. But you always knew the answers."

Yet Priya cried and felt so sad that at last the mother reached behind her pillow and pulled out a doll carved from rosewood. She gave it to Priya.

"Take this, then, Priya. It will help. When you miss me and want to ask a question, ask the doll. Let her be your friend." Then the old woman smiled weakly, closed her eyes, and changed worlds.

Priya's tears tumbled down upon her faded sari for hours until at last she picked up the doll. She stared at it. Although it was only wood, it felt good to hold.

"Doll," she said slowly, "should I prepare the body for the death rituals?"

And the doll said, "Yes, dear, do."

So Priya did what was needed and soon she sat alone in the house. She picked up the doll and said, "Doll, shall I make us some tea?"

And the doll said, "Yes, dear, do."

Priya did and felt better, so she asked, "Doll, shall I sweep the floor?"

The doll said, "Yes, dear, do." And Priya did.

Next Priya asked, "Doll, shall I cook the rice?"

"Yes, dear, do."

"Shall I grate the coconut?"

"Yes, dear, do."

"Shall I go to the bathroom?"

"YES, dear, DO!"

Days sped by, and Priya felt less lonely with her friend the doll. Then one afternoon, as she started to cook sambar soup, she saw that the fire needed feeding. But there was no wood left in the house. "Doll," she said, "we need wood. Shall we go gather some in the forest?"

The doll said yes, so Priya tucked the doll into her sari and set off across the rice fields. In the forest, Priya gathered dead branches and soon had a big bundle balanced on her head. But it was now very late, and the banyan tree, wrapped in shadows, rattled its leaves. Priya trembled as she searched for the path home.

"Doll," she whispered at last, "it's so dark, and I'm lost now. Shall we stay the night in a safe tree and go home in the morning."

The doll said, "Yes, dear, do."

So Priya hid the wood, held the doll, climbed up a sturdy tree, and at last fell asleep. Her soft snores sang through the night until suddenly she heard loud cries.

"That's MINE!"

"No, it's MINE!"

"MINE!"

Priya looked down and saw shining coins heaped like coconuts in the market. Fighting over the coins were three fierce-looking robbers. Priya knew if they found her they would kill her at once. What could she do? She picked up the doll to give her courage. She tried to think, but her fingers shook so badly that she dropped the doll. It fell straight down and hit the biggest robber right on his bald head.

"HELP!" he cried. "The soldiers have found us! They HIT me. RUN!"

The three raced off, leaving all the gold behind. Still scared, Priya waited and watched, but hours passed and they didn't return. When at last the morning sun smiled through the leaves, she felt brave enough to slide down the tree. She found her doll right on top of the pile, guarding it.

"Doll," whispered Priya, "should we take the gold home and try to find its owner?"

"Yes, dear, do," said the doll.

So Priya left with the doll and the gold. Safe at home, she locked the door and stared at the treasure. After a while she heard a loud knock on the door.

"Who is it?" she asked fearfully.

The knock was repeated, even louder.

"If I don't open, they may break the door," she thought. "I'll take a peek and scream if it's the robbers." With trembling fingers, she slid back the bolt and opened the door just a little. And there she saw . . . her husband. Happily she cried, "How good to see you! I thought you were the robbers come for the gold."

"What!" shouted Hari. "What gold, what robbers? Did you start to steal while I was away? I can't stay with a thief." Much upset, he turned to go, but Priya pulled him inside.

"Wait, husband, and listen," she said, and told him of her night's adventures.

"Priya, forgive me," said her husband. "You saved the gold that I earned. Last night three robbers stole this gold from me as I returned home through the woods. Here, thank you." And he pushed the gold toward here.

"But, husband, you earned it," she said, pushing it toward him.

"You saved it," he replied and pushed it back. Several times the gold went back and forth until finally Priya cried out. "Wait, wait, we will share this, of course!" And she picked up her doll.

"Doll," she said, "I don't think I will need you anymore for my questions. I really do know the answers myself. But I still want you as a friend. I will put you on a shelf and surround you often with fresh flowers. Before that, though, one last question. Should we share the gold and live happily ever after?"

And the doll said, "Yes, dear, do." So they did!

PLAY WITH THIS STORY

Make a paper doll of a girl from India. You can search online for "girl's clothing India" and print out a model to reproduce. On the back of your paper doll's shoulders print, "Yes, Dear, Do." Play at asking the doll a question, then bending it at the waist to reveal the answer: "Yes, Dear, Do."

Talk about how we know the right answer to our questions about how to behave. Do we need a doll to tell us that?

ABOUT THIS STORY

Cathy Spagnoli heard this story in Chennai from folklore collector Mugavai Rajamanickam. Another version is found as "Clay Mother-in-law" in *Folktales from India* by A. K. Ramanujan (New York: Pantheon, 1991), pp. 30–33. This tale includes type 1653 *Robbers under the tree. Object falls, they flee and leave money* and D1268 *Magic doll*.

THE SQUIRREL'S STRIPES

Rama's march to the island of Lanka is an exciting episode in the famous Ramayana *epic. When his army of monkeys and bears reaches the sea, they need to build a bridge to Lanka. Everyone works very hard to help, even a little squirrel.*

As the great construction of the bridge to Lanka began, Rama suddenly noticed a small squirrel. Sitting on his little feet, the squirrel watched as stones and sand were dropped into the water to make a bridge. All at once, he fell down on his back and rubbed it in the sand. Then, running on short but eager feet, the squirrel raced to the bridge, dodging the bigger animals who were working steadily.

He hopped up on the bridge and searched for cracks between the big stones. When he saw a spot where sand was needed, he shook, shook, shook his back with all his might. Sand sprinkled through the air, right into the crack.

Satisfied, the squirrel returned to the beach. He fell down once more, rubbed more sand on his back, then scurried to the bridge. There again, he shook off the sand to fill another crack. Over and over this small animal worked, all on his own, with no one but Rama even noticing him. At last he was exhausted and stopped near Rama for a moment.

"Little one, you worked so hard. Please rest," said Rama gently. As he spoke, he stroked the squirrel's back. His fingers in the soft fur made three little lines. Ever since then, many squirrels in India have three stripes running down their backs, as a reward for that squirrel's great effort. And still today those marks remind us that the hard work of even one so little can help so much.

PLAY WITH THIS STORY

Stripe a squirrel. Give each of the children a squirrel cutout and let them add three black stripes.

Repair a wall. Using boxes or blocks, build a wall. Leave cracks between the blocks. Let the children use small wads of gray paper (pebbles) and go up one at a time to stuff their pebbles in the wall.

Share Another Tale of How Squirrel Got His Stripes

"Grandfather Bear Is Hungry" in *Teaching with Story: Classroom Connections to Storytelling* by Margaret Read MacDonald, Jennifer MacDonald Whitman, and Nathaniel Forrest Whitman (Atlanta: August House, 2013). (Siberian)

How Chipmunk Got His Stripes by Joseph Bruchac, illustrated by Ariane Dewey and Jose Aruego (Turtleback, 2003). (Native American tale)

ABOUT THIS STORY

This story is retold from an incident in the *Ramayana*. It is also a version of motif A2221.8 *Squirrel's marking as reward by deity.*

ABOUT THE STORYTELLER

CATHY SPAGNOLI, writes: "Once an American storyteller, traveled overland to India, had many adventures, and met a fine young sculptor. She returned home, finished college, and sold the sculptor's batiks for an air ticket. After two and a half years, the sculptor flew to Boston on 7/7/77—a lucky day. Soon after, they married and returned to live in Cholamandal, a lovely artists' colony south of Chennai, for two years. Then they moved to Seattle, and in 1986 welcomed their marvelous son, Manu. The three live now in a house they built by themselves on Vashon Island near Seattle.

Cathy is known for her retellings of Asian folktales. She and Paramasivam and Manu have spent much time in India in their second home in Cholamandal. See her Asian folktale books, including *Terrific Trickster Tales from Asia* (Alleyside Press, 2001); *Asian Tales and Tellers* (August House, 2005); and *Nine-in-One Grr! Grr!: Folktale from the Hmong People of Laos* by Cathy Spagnoli and Blia Xong, illustrated by Nancy Hom (Childrens Book Press, 1989).

Cathy's Web site is http://www.cathyspagnoli.com.

INDONESIA

From *Indonesian Folktales* by Murti Bunanta. Edited by Margaret Read MacDonald (Libraries Unlimited, 2003).

THE SPOILED CAT

A Folktale from Deli Serdang
in North Sumatera Province

Long, long ago there lived a king who was fair and wise. He was loved by all his people. They lived sufficiently in a prosperous and peaceful kingdom. But this king had no heir.

As companions, the king kept many animals in his palace. These cheered him up considerably. But of all his animals, the king loved most his Siamese cat. So when the Siamese cat had a kitten, that kitten was completely spoiled.

One day the palace caught fire. The Siamese cat and her kitten just managed to escape into the forest. But now their life was much different than it had been at the palace. Instead of having food served to them daily on a golden platter, the mother cat now had to search everywhere for food for herself and her kitten. And instead of helping his mother, the kitten still chose to lie about waiting to be fed on a golden platter.

The poor mother cat worked hard to bring food to her kitten, but she began to suffer from the work. Though her son was no longer a baby, still she had to go out each day and find his food for him.

Seeing what a pitiful state his mother had arrived at, the son no longer considered her a suitable provider. "I will go find myself a better mother," he decided. "I need me a mother who can feed me on a golden platter as I deserve."

So the spoiled kitten set off to find a better mother.

Soon he noticed the Sun's heat and an idea occurred to him. "If the sun were my mother, my life would be very contented," he thought. So he went to the Sun.

"Dear, Sun, would you be my mother? I want to enjoy a pleasant life like yours."

But the Sun replied, "My life is pleasant. But Mist obscures me whenever it wants. Mist can make my life quite unpleasant."

"Then I want MIST for my mother," said the spoiled kitten. And he hurried off to find Mist.

"Dear, Mist, would you be my mother? I want to enjoy a pleasant life like yours."

"It is true that my life is superior to that of Sun," said Mist. "But Wind can cause me great trouble, blowing me wherever it wants. When Wind attacks me, I am blown into pieces and end by becoming mere drops of water."

"Then Wind should be my mother!" said the spoiled kitten. And off he went to seek Wind.

"Dear, Wind, would you be my mother? I want to enjoy a pleasant life like yours."

"My life is pleasant enough," said Wind. "But Hill causes me great injury. Whenever I meet Hill, I am stopped in my tracks and cannot continue my journey."

"Then I want Hill for my mother," said the spoiled kitten.

"Dear, Hill, would you be my mother? I want to have a pleasant life like yours."

"My life is pleasant some of the time," replied Hill. "But the Carabao gives me great pain. She butts and stamps my body until I am ruined and sometimes even leveled to the ground. Carabao has a better life than mine."

"Then I want Carabao for my mother," said the spoiled kitten. And he went to ask Carabao.

"Dear, Carabao, would you be my mother? I want to live a pleasant life like yours."

"Well, my life is pleasant most of the time," said Carabao. "But Rattan makes my life miserable. Rattan ties me up until I cannot move."

"Oh my. I don't want YOU for my Mother. I will ask Rattan." And the spoiled kitten went to Rattan.

"Dear, Rattan, Carabao says you can tie him up. You must be superior to Carabao. I want to live a happy life. Would you be my mother?"

"I do have a happy life," said Rattan. "But I fear Rat. Rat is my enemy. When Rat bites me the pain is unbearable. And I can be bitten into bits by that small animal."

"Then I certainly don't want *you* for my mother," said the spoiled kitten. "I want Rat!"

"Dear, Rat, would you be my mother? I want a mother who can keep me in comfort. Sun is annoyed by Mist. Mist is scattered by Wind. Wind is blocked by Hill. Hill is trampled by Carabao. Carabao is tied by Rattan. Rattan is gnawed to bits by Rat. You, Rat, are superior. You can provide me with a life of comfort such as I wish."

"All this is true," said Rat. "Yet there is one who makes my life miserable too. In this forest there lives a thin, old cat. She tracks my every move. One day she will catch me, and I will die."

Suddenly the spoiled kitten realized just who the thin, old cat must be.

"Do you mean the old cat who lives alone in the middle of the woods?"

"Exactly. That is the old cat I fear," replied Rat.

"But that is my OWN mother!" cried the spoiled kitten.

And rushing home, he begged his mother's forgiveness and settled down to be a good son. He realized now that if he was to find happiness, it must be with his own mother.

Fortunately the kitten now lost his spoiled ways and became a diligent and obedient child. Now that there were two of them to share the work, he and his mother lived a happy and comfortable life in their forest home.

PLAY WITH THIS STORY

Create felt board fun. Make simple outline patterns for sun, cloud, wind, mountain, carabao (buffalo), rattan grasses, and rat and cut these from felt. Let the children retell the story using a cat puppet while putting the felt characters on a felt board. You can make a flannel board or felt board by covering a large piece of cardboard with flannel or gluing a large piece of felt to a cardboard.

Compare and Contrast

This motif appears in many variants around the world. Read other tales with this motif to your children and compare them. Picture books with this theme include the following:

The Wedding of the Rat Family by Caroll Kendall (New York: Macmillan, 1988). (China)
The Mouse Bride: A Mayan Folktale by Judith Dupré (New York: Knopf, 1993). (Maya)
Mouse Match: A Chinese Folktale by Ed Young (San Diego: Harcourt, Brace, 1997). (China)
The Rat's Daughter by Joel Cook (Honesdale, PA: Boyds Mills, 1993). (Japan)
The Greatest of All by Eric Kimmel (New York: Holiday House, 1991). (Japan)
The Moles and the Mireuk by Holly H. Kwon (New York: Houghton Mifflin, 1993). (Korea)

Share Similar Stories

Stonecutter wishes self higher:
The Stonecutter: A Japanese Folktale by Gerald McDermott (New York: Viking, 1975). You can view the five-minute video of McDermott's animated film *The Stonecutter* at https://archive.org/details/afana_stonecutter. (Japan)
Two Stonecutters by Eve Titus (Garden City, NY: Doubleday, 1967). (Japan)
The Stonecutter by Demi (New York: Crown, 1995). (China)
Kantchil's Lime Pit and Other Stories of Indonesia by Harold Courlander (New York: Harcourt, Brace, 1950), pp. 96–100. (Indonesia)

Girl to wed most powerful person in world:
Twenty-Five Fables by Norah Montgomerie (New York: Abelard-Schuman, 1964), pp. 41–43. (India)
Ant loses foot to frost, attacks snow, sun, etc.:

Three Wishes: A Collection of Puerto Rican Folktales by Ricardo Alegría (New York: Harcourt, Brace & World, 1969), pp. 40–43. (Puerto Rico)
The Tiger and the Rabbit and Other Tales by Pura Belpré (Philadelphia: Lippincott, 1965), pp. 57–61. (Puerto Rico)

Thrush blames frost for wounded foot, frost blames sun, etc.:
Folktales of Chile by Yolanda Pino-Saavedra (Chicago: University of Chicago, 1967), pp. 245–246. (Chile)

Boy thinks self strongest until slips on ice:
The Parent's Guide to Storytelling by Margaret Read MacDonald (August House, 2005), pp. 62–66.
   (Siberia, Amur River)

ABOUT THIS STORY

This is motif Z42 *Stronger and strongest* and motif L392 *Mouse stronger than wall, wind, mountain.*

WHY SHRIMPS ARE CROOKED
A Folktale from Central Kalimantan Province

In Central Kalimantan people perform the tradition of mandep, a kind of shared work. It means that if some-one is doing a large-scale work, such as building a house or harvesting rice, they will be doing mandep or receiving mandep. More or less, mandep means to help, and andep means a help. Therefore, if someone has ever helped someone else, in turn he or she will get help also when doing something.

This following folktale tells about the tradition of mandep through a story about a school of fish.

A long time ago, there was once a school of fish who wanted to do large-scale work. Each of them planned to open a farm. Therefore, they decided that each in turn would help the other.

The idea first came from the *gabus* fish. His best friend, the *miau* fish, often came to visit him. They were heard talking.

"My brother *miau* fish, what is your opinion about the forest fire that just happened?" asked the *gabus* fish to the *miau* fish.

"What do you think?" asked the *miau* fish in return.

"I think it would be good if we use the burned area for a huge farm, as we don't need to cut and chop down the trees," replied the *gabus* fish.

"Your idea really does make sense!" answered the *miau* fish.

"So, won't it be better if we also invite other fish to have a meeting to discuss our plan? Thus, we can open a bigger farm," suggested the *gabus* fish.

"It is really a good idea. I agree with you. Let us invite the *saluang* fish, the *banta* fish, the *masaw* fish, and the others so that we can realize this work."

So the *gabus* and *miau* fish went to the house of each fish. They all were happy to hear the *gabus* fish's idea. All of them gladly responded and promised to come to the meeting the *gabus* fish was going to hold.

On a fixed day everyone gathered. There came also *balida, tabiring, manjuhan, patin, lawang, kakapar, bapuyu, sepat, lele, telan,* and many kinds of scaly fishes and, not to be left out, the shrimp.

After all the invited fishes gathered, the *gabus* fish started the discussion, "Brothers, today we gather to discuss a big work that needs to be shared. We are going to open a farm in the forest in the place where it has been burnt down. Therefore, we need a chairman who will organize this work so that we can do it well."

All the fish agreed to what the *gabus* fish said. Among them there was *masaw* fish. He stood up and said, "I think *tabiring* fish is the most appropriate to be the chairman."

Apparently *lele* fish didn't really agree. He then proposed his candidate, "Brother *tabiring* is strong, but we could also ask brother *tambahan* to be the chairman."

Hurly-burly, the fishes proposed candidate after candidate. But still they could not decide who was the most appropriate to be the chairman.

After refusing many candidates, finally *saluang* fish was chosen. *Saluang* fish stood in the middle of the crowd and decided that the work had to start on the following day.

In the morning, they left for the place where they wanted to work. Each of them stuck a pole as a sign of the border of the farm they owned.

The fish soon cleaned up the woods in their farm. Afterwards they used sticks to make holes for planting the seeds. For making the holes they needed a lot of people to help, so they made arrangements for whose farm would be prepared for planting first.

So it was, on the first day the fish prepared *manjuhan*'s farm. While the others were at work, the *manjuhan* fish prepared the food.

Soon he started to cook because there were a lot of fish who were doing *mandep*. The *manjuhan*'s farm was large. After cooking rice, he prepared the dishes. He considered for a while. Then he took a big cooking pot and filled it with cold water.

What did he do? He entered the pot. Not long after *manjuhan* jumped out again from the pot. Apparently he laid eggs there.

He then placed the pot which had been filled with eggs on a hearth. Afterwards he put a lot of vegetables in it.

At noon, all the fishes went back to the hut to take a rest and have lunch. "*Manjuhan*, how delicious the smell of your food! What kind of dish did you cook?" asked the fish.

"Look by yourselves and enjoy my cooking," replied *Manjuhan*. After a while the rice and the dish were done. All the fishes ate together. How delicious was the food *Manjuhan* prepared.

After they ate, *kakapar* and *bapuyu* fish were talking about the delicacy of *Manjuhan*'s food. "*Bapuyu*, how clever is *Manjuhan*. Do you know how he cooked the food?" asked *kakapar* fish.

Bapuyu was silent for a while. He tried to think. "Well, *Kakapar*," said *Bapuyu*, "before the dish was placed on the hearth, when the pot was just filled with water, *Manjuhan* entered into the pot and laid eggs there."

"What you said is right," answered *Kakapor*. "I also thought the same thing about how *Manjuhan* cooked. How really clever he is."

After lunch, the fishes went back to work until the day had become almost dark. After finishing, before they went home, *Manjuhan* served the delicious food again.

After they had prepared *Manjuhan*'s farm, the fishes moved to *Balida*'s. It was the same at *Balida*'s farm. He prepared a food as delicious as the food *Manjuhan* had prepared.

Now it was the turn of *tabiring* fish to get help. At *Tabiring*'s place they also were served with food not less delicious than the food *Manjuhan* had prepared.

So it happened. They prepared each of the farms in turn, until eventually they came to the shrimp's.

Before they started to work, the *gabus* fish asked the shrimp, "Shrimp, what dishes will be for us today?"

"You do not need to worry. For sure it will be as delicious as the previous," answered the shrimp, smiling.

Do you know how to cook?" asked the *gabus* fish.

"Everything will be fine. If they can do it, I surely can!" replied the shrimp, very sure of himself.

While the others were preparing the farm, the shrimp prepared the food. He then set the fire in the hearth to cook rice. After a while it was done.

"Well," he said to himself, "how do I cook the delicious meal like all friends did?"

He thought for a while, then he took a big cooking pot and filled it with water. Afterwards, he placed it on a hearth. Not long after, the water in it started to boil. The smoke of the boiled water billowed. Suddenly, "plung," the shrimp jumped into the cooking pot.

Noon passed and the shrimp still had not called his friends to go back to the hut. All of them were waiting, but even when the sun had set in the west, there was no call from the shrimp.

"What has happened? Why is the shrimp so late? I am starving!" said the *masaw* fish.

"Yes, I am hungry, too," said the *banta* fish.

All the fishes grumbled. Until the day had become dark there was no call from the shrimp. Finally, the *saluang* fish suggested that they stop for a while, "Friends, let us go back to the hut first and see what the shrimp is doing."

So it was, the fishes went back to the hut with nagging stomachs, restraining their hunger.

Arriving at the hut, the *saluang* fish called up, "Shrimp, shrimp, has the food been ready?" But no one answered.

"What has actually happened to shrimp?" asked the fishes to each other.

Immediately they looked into the hut. The fire in the hearth had already died out. The cooking pot was still on it. Even the rice which was done hadn't been taken out.

They all wondered, "Where is shrimp?" They called him. But the shrimp didn't answer at all.

After searching everywhere and not finding shrimp, they started to eat. First they spooned the rice; afterwards each of them took the dish. Nothing strange happened.

But when the *patin* fish took the dish, suddenly he saw shrimp among the vegetables. His body was crooked, reddish, and he was already dead. All the fish were in an uproar after learning that the shrimp was dead and his body crooked among the vegetables.

This was what had happened to the shrimp, because of his stupidity in not asking the other fish how to prepare food. His stupidity caused his death.

People say that ever since that time, when a shrimp dies, its body will become crooked. This will not happen to the fishes, though.

PLAY WITH THIS STORY

Pay attention to directions. Talk about the importance of asking directions if you are not sure of yourself. Tell stories about a time you did not follow directions and got in trouble. Ask the children to tell about a time this happened to them.

Have a shrimp treat. Serve cold-boiled shrimp as a treat. Note: please be sure to check for food allergies before offering any food to children.

Why Shrimps Are Crooked

Act it out. Assign fish roles and act out this story.

Tell another know-it-all tale. See also "Know-It-All Tangik" on page 1.

ABOUT THIS STORY

This is motif J2401 *Fatal imitation*; motif J2415.3 *Crab tries to imitate bird who lays eggs in pot of boiling water. Falls in instead of being rewarded*; and motif A2411.5.7 *Color of shrimp*.

A Note from the Author

I grew up in Semarang, the capital town of Central Java. This town is famous for its rich varieties of food: a mixture of Javanese and Chinese. During my childhood, when I was at the elementary school, my mother used to tell classic folktales that are mostly known up to now. Dozens of stories I have heard from my mother. I love folktales because of the way she told the stories with no intention to teach any morals but just to share the stories. When I wrote my own books I also retold other beautiful stories that I heard from friends or from my desk research. And again, I also just want to share stories. Good stories will tell for themselves whether they contain morals or entertainment.

Storytelling lies deeply in the Indonesian tradition as a vehicle to educate younger generations and communities. It is presented in many forms, such as theater, musical dance, puppet theaters, individual performances, and so on. It is worth noting that folktale books are still the favorite publications for the Indonesian publishing houses. But it is a pity that many are not well written and present only the same stories that are already known. That was why I always try to refine new good stories that can be shared by everybody and have been rarely heard before. So you will get fresh stories.

ABOUT THE AUTHOR

DR. MURTI BUNANTA is the organizer of KPBA, Kelampok Pencinta Bacaan Anak, the Indonesian division of IBBY, The International Board of Books for Youth. She has produced over 30 folktale picture books for publication in Indonesia. Her KPBA team present storytelling programs and teacher workshops throughout Indonesia.

ABOUT THE EDITOR

Margaret Read Macdonald has visited Jakarta multiple times to tell stories for Murti Bunanta's KPBA group. She has traveled with them throughout Indonesia, and has coached them in performing many of the stories in Murti's book, *Indonesian Folktales*.

JAPAN

From *Folktales from the Japanese Countryside by Hiroko Fujita. Edited* by Fran Stallings (Libraries Unlimited, 2008).

SPOOKY TANUKI MUSIC

Many stories are told of the tanuki badgers playing music by pounding on their fat little bellies in the moonlight. Here is one.

Once upon a time, there was a temple deep, deep in the mountains. Every night the temple's priest was haunted by spooky noises. He couldn't bear it, and he resigned.

The next priest was a jolly man. "Spooky or not, it's better to hear something than no sound at all. Well, what kind of noise will it be?"

The new priest waited for evening to fall. He sat in the middle of the main hall and finished his evening prayer. Then he kept sitting there.

After midnight it started. From the mountain behind the temple came a deep thumping sound: *Po-n!*

"Oh, I heard that strange noise! But just one! Well, why did it stop?" he wondered. Then, from the other direction, came a light tapping sound: *Poko, poko.* "I hear it," said the priest.

> *Po-n, poko, poko. Po-n, poko, poko.*
> From here, *Po-n!*
> From there, *Po-n!*
> From over there, *Poko, poko, poko, poko.*

The sounds became louder and louder. They were coming closer and closer to the temple.

> *Po-n, poko, poko.*

The priest started to enjoy it. When he heard *po-n*, he rang his prayer gong: *Chi-n!* When he heard *poko, poko*, he beat his wood block: *Poku, poku.*

> *Po-n, chi-n! Poko, poko, poku, poku!*
> *Po-n, chi-n! Poko, poko, poku, poku!*

It seemed like the noise makers were gathering in the temple garden.

Po-n, chi-n! Poko, poko, poku, poku!
Po-n, chi-n! Poko, poko, poku, poku!
Po-n, chi-n! Poko, poko, poku, poku!
Po-n, chi-n! Poko, poko, poku, poku!

It was such fun.

The priest got more and more excited. "What is making this sound?" he wondered. "I will see what it is."

The priest stopped ringing his gong and moved quietly toward the window. When he looked out, those who were in the temple garden scattered away toward the mountain. Maybe it's because the priest stopped his part, or maybe it's because they noticed him opening the window. Anyway, the next evening the priest opened the window a little in advance and waited. After midnight, he heard the sound again: *Po-n, poko, poko.* It sounded like more and more noises were gathering.

Po-n, poko, poko.
Po-n, poko, poko.
Po-n, poko, poko.

More and more were gathering in the temple garden.

The priest looked. They were a group of tanuki.

"Very well. I will join in." But then he thought, "I have to stop my gong and wood block if I want to see them. If I stop, they might run away again like yesterday. Tonight, instead of gong and wood block, I will use my belly."

So, at *po-n* from the garden, he thumped his belly: *Becha.* At *poko, poko* from the garden, he tapped his belly: *Pita, pita.*

Po-n. Becha.
Poko, poko. Pita, pita.
Po-n, becha. Poko, poko, pita, pita.
Po-n, becha, poko, poko, pita, pita.
Po-n, becha, poko, poko, pita, pita.

It was such fun.

Po-n, becha, poko, poko, pita, pita.
Po-n, becha, poko, poko, pita, pita.

The tanuki were all enjoying it very much, too.

But after a while, everyone's bellies became red and started to hurt. In the end, they were all rubbing their bellies.

"This is very much fun," the priest told the tanuki, "but we can't do this every night. If we do, our bellies might burst. Why don't we do it only on the night of a full moon?"

He wasn't sure if they understood him. Without saying anything, the tanuki just went back to the mountain.

But he didn't hear anything the next night, and the next night, and the next.

On the next full moon night, the priest waited eagerly. From the mountain, he heard it.

Po-n.
Poko, poko.
Po-n, poko, poko.
Po-n, poko, poko.

They were gathering in the garden. The priest went out to the garden, too. When the tanuki went *po-n*, the priest went *becha*. When they went *poko, poko*, he went *pita, pita*. And from then on, on full moon nights, the villagers could hear from the temple:

Po-n, becha, poko, poko, pita, pita.
Po-n, becha, poko, poko, pita, pita.
Oshimai!

PLAY WITH THIS STORY

Play some Japanese music. Choose music with a good beat. Dance in a circle and pound your tummies to make thumping music. One person might be the priest and ring a bell, "chi-n," and tap a wooden block, "poku, poku."

ABOUT THIS STORY

Badgers are known for their ability to play on their tummies to make drum music. Hiroko tells us that sometimes the story ends with the badgers trying to see who can bang the loudest. They beat their tummies until their tummies burst. Dead tanuki are found on the ground the next morning.

Another interesting tale of the tanuki is found in *The Very Special Badgers* by Claus Stamm (New York: Viking, 1960).

MOUSE TEETH

Millet is a small-seeded cereal grain used to make tasty dumplings, noodles, and other dishes.

Once upon a time, there was a weasel who decided to grow millet to store for winter. In the spring, he turned over the soil and planted the millet seeds. He took great care of them.

When autumn came, his field was full of ripe millet. The heads of grain were as thick as a tanuki's tail. Weasel was very happy at the sight.

"I will harvest the millet tomorrow," he thought, and went home.

The next day, when he came to his field to harvest his millet, it was already gone.

"Oh, who took my millet? I worked very hard, and it grew so well. Who had the nerve to steal it?" He was furious.

He searched from one house to another. He walked and walked until he heard tiny voices coming from a burrow.

"It was so tasty, last night's millet cake.

"It was so tasty, last night's millet cake."

Weasel pricked up his ears. "Well, what's this?"

A small mouse came out of the burrow scampering *choro choro chorori* singing, "It was so tasty, last night's millet cake."

The next little mouse came out *choro choro chorori* singing, "It was so tasty, last night's millet cake."

Another came *choro choro chorori*. "It was so tasty, last night's millet cake."

Then, out came a big mouse. "Hush! Hush! Don't sing such a song outside," she said to her children.

Now Weasel understood. He started digging from the other side of the burrow. He dug and dug and found a pile of millet hidden at the very end of the mouse burrow.

Weasel was furious. He caught Mother Mouse.

"Why did you steal my millet? I worked so hard to grow it!" He was almost ready to kill the mouse.

"Oh, oh, I'm very sorry. I just wanted to feed my children. I'm very sorry. You can take all the rest. Please forgive me," Mother Mouse said.

Weasel got all the rest of his millet back, but he was still angry. "I'll kill this mouse!" He was going to bite her.

"Please, don't kill me. Oh, please! I must take care of my babies!" Mother Mouse begged.

He let her live, but he was still angry. "I will cut off your teeth so that you can't steal more millet!" He got his saw and prepared to cut off all her teeth.

She said, "Yes, I did wrong. You have a right to cut off my teeth. But if I lose all my teeth, I can't gnaw a hole through the wall of the storage building at the manor house. Just two teeth would be very much appreciated. Please leave two teeth for me."

Weasel started to feel pity. He decided to leave two front teeth on her upper jaw and two on her lower jaw. All the rest he cut off with his saw.

That's why mice have only two teeth in the front of each jaw.

But Weasel's mercy was his ruin. He stored his recovered millet at the very end of his house. Little by little, it seemed to disappear.

When he checked the room carefully, he found a tiny hole in the wall. The teeth he left for the mouse were so strong that even with only two pairs of front teeth, she could gnaw a hole through wood, packed earth, or anything.

Oshimai!

TELLING THIS STORY

Hiroko Fujita writes:

For very young listeners, you can add actions and audience participation:

Weasel plowed the field. [Pretend to plow; encourage young listeners to mirror you.]
Weasel sowed millet seeds. [Pretend to sow.]
Weasel weeded. [Pretend to pull up weeds.]
The millet grew well. [Raise right hand and then left hand.]
The ripe millet heads swung heavily. [Wave both hands.]
Weasel reaped the millet. [Pretend to reap the millet stalks.]
Weasel bundled them up. [Pretend to bundle them up.]
Weasel carried the bundles home. [Pretend to carry them on your shoulder.]
Weasel put them away. [Pretend to close doors.]

"Now, I'm all prepared for the winter. I will take a nap." [Press hands together and put them on the side of your face.]
"Ahh, I'm awake now. I'm hungry." [Yawn and pat your stomach.]
"I will eat my millet." [Pretend to open the doors.]
"Oh, no! No millet! No millet! No millet! No millet!"

[Listeners, in the roles of other animals, can reply in this pattern:]

Weasel: Dog, Dog, did you steal my millet?
Dog: I never steal. Wan wan (Bow wow).
Weasel: That's right. You don't steal. Cat, Cat, did you steal my millet?
Cat: I never steal. Niau, niau (Meow meow).

Weasel: That's right. You don't steal. Pig, Pig, did you steal my millet?
Pig: I never steal. Bu bu (Oink, oink).
Weasel: That's right. You don't steal.

[—and so forth. Participating "animals" can add, "I eat bones/fish/scraps," etc. Then you can proceed with the mouse part of the story.]

You can elaborate the story taking a lot of time using Hiroko's suggestions above. And she writes:

When you sing, "It was so tasty, last night's millet cake," I would like you to create a suitable melody. To make it sound like a children's song, you should emphasize the natural tones of speech and give it some rhythm.

PLAY WITH THIS STORY

Talk about customs surrounding mice and the loss of baby teeth. Hiroko Fujita writes:

It is not the custom any more, but at the time when my baby teeth were coming out, we sang, "Exchange this tooth with a mouse tooth." We threw the tooth up on to the roof if it was a lower tooth, and down into the space under the floor if it was an upper tooth. We wanted the new tooth to grow in as strong as mouse teeth.

There were many mice in the house where I lived in Fukushima. At night, I could hear them running around in the attic. It was as if they were having a Sports Day every day. In the kitchen, in the closet, there were mouse holes. We tried to fight them by stuffing the holes with cedar leaves or nailing boards over the holes. But soon we found new holes right beside the stuffing. Mice really have strong teeth.

In Europe a child's lost tooth is sometimes taken by a mouse, Raton Perez, in Spain, for example, or Le Petite Souris, in France. You can find out about other tooth-loss traditions around the world in books such as *Throw Your Tooth on the Roof: Tooth Traditions from Around the World* by Selby Beeler, illustrated by G. Brian Karas (Boston: HMH Books for Young Readers, 2013)

ABOUT THIS STORY

The Japanese folklorist Hiroko Ikeda has classified this as Ikeda 2048 *The Weasel's Millet*. Many Japanese versions of this story begin with Weasel and Mouse agreeing to raise the millet crop together, then mouse claims to be sick and comes back to eat. This is Type 9 *The Unjust Partner*. In some versions, Weasel asks many animals if they stole it.

Yanagita Kunio gives several versions of this story as story #324 in *The Yanagito Kunio Guide to the Japanese Folk Tale*, edited and translated by Fanny Hagin Mayer (Bloomington, IN: Indiana University Press, 1986).

ABOUT THE AUTHORS

HIROKO FUJITA is an early childhood educator in Japan and travels extensively sharing her folktales in schools, libraries, and community centers. She is author of over 24 books in Japanese. In English, she has published *Stories to Play With*, adapted and edited by Fran Stallings (August House, 2005); *How to Fool a Cat: Japanese Folktales for Children* (Parkhurst Brothers, 2015); and *The Price of Three Stories: Rare Folktales from Japan* (Parkhurst Brothers, 2015).

Hiroko grew up in the rural mountain town of Miharu in Fukushima Prefecture. There she heard folktales told by Mr. Takeda Kuni, a farmer who worked the field next to her family's two-room cabin. She also heard tales from elders in her family and in the households of school friends. Later, as a young woman in Fukushima City, she heard more tales from Mrs. Toshiko Endo, an elder from rural Fukushima Prefecture.

FRAN STALLINGS is a professional storyteller and writer from Bartlesville, Oklahoma. Fran arranges annual storytelling tours to the United States for Hiroko and tours with Hiroko in Japan. She has collaborated with Hiroko on *Stories to Play With*, *How to Fool a Cat*, and *The Price of Three Stories* above.

Fran's Web site is http://www.franstallings.com.

KENYA

From *Hyena and the Moon: Stories to Tell from Kenya* by Heather McNeil (Libraries Unlimited, 1994).

NOT SO!

A long time ago, nobody ever listened to Ground Squirrel. Now, Ground Squirrel was *mdogo sana*, very small. But he was also *akili sana*, very clever. His name was Kidiri, and this is his story.

There came a time when Mama Simba, the mother of the lions, had two babies, *watoto wawili*. Oh, she was so proud! She took her babies to the water hole, and all day she bragged about how her babies would be the handsomest, the fastest, the strongest of all the animals.

Mama Nyani, the mother of the baboons, heard all the bragging, and she was not impressed. She gathered her own two babies onto her back, where she knew they would be safe. Then she climbed up into a tree and called down to the lion, "Hey, Mama Simba! What makes you think your babies are so special? Look at them! What can they do? They growl like frogs, they sleep like lazy hyenas, and they fall over their feet like clumsy beetles!"

When the animals heard this, they laughed and laughed—except for Mama Simba. The mother of the lions did not laugh, and the mother of the lions did not forget.

Later that day, Mama Nyani went down to the water hole to get a drink of *maji*, water. While she was gone, her babies played roll-and-tumble and hide-and-jump and catch-a-tail. And all the time that they were playing, they did not realize they were being watched. Hiding in the bushes was Mama Simba. She waited until the baby baboons came rolling and tumbling by, and then—THWACK! THWACK!—she held a baby baboon under each of her front paws. Oh, such a screeching and hollering they made, and that brought Mama Nyani running back from the water hole.

"*Watoto wangu!* My babies! Let my babies go!"

"What are you talking about, Mama Nyani? These are not your babies. These are my babies."

"What are *you* talking about, Mama Simba? How could they be your babies?"

"They are with me, are they not? So they must be mine."

"Those babies have thick, brown fur, the color of mud. You have fur the color of grass. Those babies have arms like vines so they can swing in the trees. You do not swing in the trees. Those babies have hands like human hands. You have the paws, the claws, the fangs of a cat. Let my babies go!"

"Very well, Mama Nyani. I will let these babies go if there is one animal here who will stand in front of me, look into *macho yangu*, my eyes, and say these are not my children. Which one of you animals will say this to me?"

Nyamaza. Silence. There was not one animal who would walk up to the mother of the lions, look into her eyes, and call her a liar. Except Kidiri! The little ground squirrel knew the babies belonged to Mama Nyani, so he called out. "Not so! Not so! It is not so!"

But, as usual, no one heard Kidiri.

So he puffed out his chest, and a little bit louder he called out, "Not so! Not so! It is not so!"

Still, no one heard Kidiri.

The little ground squirrel stood up tall on his toes, puffed out his chest, and yelled as loud as he could, "NOT SO! NOT SO! IT IS NOT SO!"

But still, no one heard Kidiri.

So now he ran—plippity, plippity, plip—over to Mama Nyani and began to pull on her leg. The mother of the baboons looked down and very annoyed, cried, "Hey, Kidiri! What are you doing? What do you want?"

The little ground squirrel stood up tall, puffed out his chest, and called out, "Not so! Not so! It is not so!"

"What's that?" said Mama Nyani. "What did you say?"

"Not so! Not so! It is not so!"

"Oh *rafiki mdogo wangu*! My little friend! You must say that to Mama Simba!"

"But she will not hear me. And I'm not going to pull on her leg! But I have an idea. You and the other baboons must build me a tall mound of dirt, so tall that when I stand on the top, I can look into *macho ya simba*, the eyes of the lion. Then you must dig *shimo*, a hole, all the way down the middle of the mound of dirt and into the earth below."

So Mama Nyani called together all the baboons, and, with their hands like human hands, they built the mound of dirt. Then they dug *shimo* down through the middle of the mound and into the earth below.

Kidiri climbed to the top of the mound of dirt, looked directly into *macho ya simba*, and called out, "Not so! Not so! It is not so!"

"*What* did you say, Kidiri?"

The little ground squirrel gulped with fear. "Not so? Not so! It is not so! Those babies with dark brown fur, those babies with arms like vines, those babies with hands like human hands, those are the babies of Mama Nyani!" And—PLIP!—Kidiri disappeared down into the hole.

"RAAWR!" Mama Simba leaped forward to grab the ground squirrel, and as she did so, she lifted up her front paws, and—WHISH!—the two baby baboons ran back to their mother. But the mother of the lions was not going to let the ground squirrel get away, too. With her paw, she reached down into the hole, but she could not reach far enough. So she called for

Tembo, the Elephant, and using his trunk, Tembo reached down, down, down, into the hole until his trunk wrapped around the leg of Kidiri.

Kidiri could feel himself being pulled back up the hole towards the angry lion, but remember, he was not only *mdogo sana*, he was also *akili sana*. Kidiri called out, "Oh, silly Tembo. You think you are pulling my leg? You are not pulling my leg. You are pulling . . . you are pulling . . . you are pulling the root of a tree!"

So Tembo let go of what he thought was the root of a tree, and he felt all around with his trunk until it wrapped around . . . the root of a tree! And while Tembo pulled and pulled on what he thought was the leg of the ground squirrel, and while Mama Simba paced and paced in front of the mound of dirt waiting for the little ground squirrel to appear, Kidiri dug his way through to his tunnels in the earth, and he ran away, laughing and saying, "Not so! Not so! It is not so!"

TELLING THIS STORY

Heather McNeil suggests using voices to match the temperament of the various animals. "Baboon, often the evil pest in Kenyan folktales, is brazen and loud. Lion is strong, and self-assured and has all the time in the world. Ground Squirrel, like the trickster Rabbit, is small, nervous, and clever out of necessity."

The audience can be encouraged to join in on Ground Squirrel's insistent "Not so! Not so! IT IS NOT SO!"

PLAY WITH THIS STORY

Sort out baby animals. Photocopy pictures of mother and baby animals (or cut them from magazines). Place the pictures in a pile and let the children match mothers to babies and paste them onto a mural paper together.

Play calling your baby game. Give each child a picture of either a mother or baby animal. Mothers form a circle. Babies are in the middle. Each mother makes her call, and her babies make an answering call and run to stand behind her. Put the pictures back in a pile in the middle of the circle. Each child selects a picture, and the game repeats.

ABOUT THIS STORY

Motif K543 *Biting the foot. Fox to bear, who is biting his foot: "You are biting the tree root."* MacDonald and Sturm's *Storyteller's Sourcebook* (2000) gives variants of this motif from India as well as other Kenyan sources. MacDonald's *Storyteller's Sourcebook* (1982) gives African American variants as well as variants from Ceylon, Africa: Yoruba, Indonesia, Malaysia, Bangladesh, Pakistan, and Europe.

Heather McNeil visited some Turkana families to hear their stories. She tells us: "The grandmother and her two female friends sat on a grass mat, singing and clapping a song of welcome. . . .

The women giggled and punched each other, one sometimes interrupting and taking the story from another. . . . The accompanying rituals of finger snapping, chanting, and hand clapping were wonderful." In her book *Hyena and Moon,* Heather gives two versions of this story: one Turkana and one Samburu. She says she actually heard many versions of this story. Sometimes the babies were stolen from an ostrich, a mongoose, or a ground squirrel.

You will find it useful and interesting to read Heather's book, in which she tells of her travels in Kenya and talks of her story listening experiences. She retells all of the stories in a tellable format, but she also gives the original text as it was heard from the Kenyan traditional teller.

ABOUT THE AUTHOR

HEATHER MCNEIL became interested in Kenya when she was a child and read the trilogy of *Born Free* books by Joy Adamson. She spent the next 30 years researching the animals and cultures of Kenya, and finally fulfilled a lifelong dream when she traveled with a member of the Kikuyu people, collecting stories and relishing sunrise safaris with cheetahs, flamingoes and all the magnificence of Kenya.

Heather is a third-generation storyteller, following the tradition of her grandfather, aunt, and mother. She is currently the Youth Services Manager for Deschutes Public Library in Bend, Oregon, where she lives with her daughter, horse, and many wonderful memories of hearing stories around a campfire while lions roared and hyenas whooped in the distance.

KOREA

From *A Tiger by the Tail and Other Stories from the Heart of Korea.* Retold by Lindy Soon Curry. Edited by Chan-eung Park (Libraries Unlimited, 1999).

THE CHARMING FLUTE

There once was a woodcutter who played a Korean flute with such great skill that he was able to express his every mood with the flute. He played soulful sounds when he was mourning a loss. He played soothing sounds to calm people and put them to sleep. But mostly he was a happy person and played joyful and merry tunes. He liked to play his flute wherever he went, especially as he went to the forest to chop wood. As he played, the birds flocked around him and harmonized with him. Children gathered around him and sang and danced as he played in the meadow.

He was in a fine, playful mood one day when he was rudely confronted by a large, ferocious tiger. Just before the tiger leaped toward him, the man spotted a tall tree and scrambled up it as fast as he could. The tiger tried to climb the tree after him but was not able to. It tried several times but finally gave up and disappeared into the thick forest.

The woodcutter was much relieved but was still in such a state of shock that he was not able to come down out of the tree. He just sat there trying to calm himself. Soon the tiger returned with several other tigers to help him capture the man.

One tiger stood next to the tree while a second climbed on top of him, then a third climbed on top of the second. The fourth tiger climbed on top of the tower of tigers and was within reach of the poor woodcutter.

At this the woodcutter decided to accept his fate and die happily and joyfully. So he took up his flute and began to play the merriest tune he had ever played. The tiger on the bottom happened to be very musical and loved to dance to music. He swayed and pranced to the rhythm. As he danced, the other tigers struggled to keep balance, but they quickly tumbled down and the whole tower toppled over.

Noticing what was happening, the woodcutter played faster and faster. When all the tigers except the dancing tiger had fallen to the ground unconscious, the woodcutter quietly slipped down from the tree and ran into the village still playing his flute. He only stopped playing when he knew he was safe. And thus, the woodcutter's life was saved by his charming flute.

PLAY WITH THIS STORY

Act it out. The flute player sits on a tabletop (in the tree). The other children are tigers and surround the table while the flute player plays a slide whistle or simple flute. The tigers place their hands on the shoulders of the tigers in front of them. Then one by one the tigers peel off from the group and begin to dance until all are dancing. The flute player gets down and tiptoes away, playing all the while. Choose a different flute player (or two or three flute players) and repeat.

ABOUT THIS STORY

Motif D1415.2 *Magical musical instrument causes person to dance.*

MacDonald cites many tales under this motif, including magic horn (Denmark); magic flute (Portugal, Russia-Altai, Yugoslavia); magic pipe (Bulgaria, Ireland, Latvia, Spain); magic fiddle (Germany, Luxembourg); magic lute (Russia); and magic drum (Congo -Luban, Korea). The Korean variant is from *Which Was Witch? Tales of Ghosts and Magic from Korea* by Eleanore Myers Jewett (New York: Viking, 1953), pp. 136–157, and *The Story Bag: A Collection of Korean Folk Tales* by So-Un Kim (Rutland, VT: Tuttle, 1955), pp. 186–198. It includes a hand drum that causes people to dance when beaten. MacDonald and Sturm cite variants about pipes (Ireland); fiddle (Jamaica, Cajun, Germany); drums (Sierra Leone); and marimba (Sotho, Swazi).

This is also similar to K606.2.0.5 *Escape by persuading captors to dance.* Stories on this motif appear throughout the world. MacDonald and Sturm cite versions from Indonesia, Sierra Leone, South Africa, Eskimo, Haiti, Cherokee, Athabaskan, Brazil, The Antilles, and Zimbabwe (Shona). MacDonald adds Byelorussian and Makah variants.

For another dancing tale, see "The Poor Lady's Plan" on page 141 (Saudi Arabia).

ABOUT THE STORYTELLER

Lindy Soon Curry was adopted at age four from an orphanage in Korea. She grew up in Mt. Hood, Oregon, but always longed to connect with her Korean heritage. She has been telling stories since 1990 and received a Colorado Asian Woman of Achievement Award in 1995. From her research and her years of storytelling, she has prepared *A Tiger by the Tail and Other Stories from the Heart of Korea.*

KURDISH

From *A Fire in My Heart: Kurdish Tales*. Retold by Diane Edgecomb. With contributions by Mohammed M. A. Ahmed and Cheto Ozel. Libraries Unlimited, 2008.

EYES OF A CAT

One day, the cats decided to change their ways, to stop torturing mice and oppressing them. They announced that they would now travel in the path of religion, tolerance, and peace. When the mice heard about this they were very happy, but they were still suspicious. "We will wait and see what happens," they said. "We have been waiting for this for centuries."

The cats sent a representative to the mice.

"We cats are tired of chasing you around and around," the representative said. "We would like to sign a peace agreement with you."

"Yes, we would like this too," responded the mice. "We are tired of escaping just as you are tired of chasing."

"Well then, let there be peace. You can prove that you trust us by closing up all of the holes and tunnels that you use to escape. As for us, to prove that we have changed our ways, we are going on a pilgrimage to Mecca. On our return you will see that we will never attack you."

So the cats went to the holy land. While they were there, they prayed and swore never to eat mice again. They did all the things they had to do to get away from their sinful ways. After they finished their prayers, they lined up and came back home.

Of course, on their return, everyone went to visit them and welcome them. They were important now because whoever travels to Mecca is considered to be holy as well. Everyone who went to see them gave them a good report.

The mice heard the news that the cats had returned. But the mice didn't want to listen to rumors that the cats had changed their ways, they wanted to see it with their own eyes. The leaders of the mice held a meeting, and they assigned a delegation of mice to go and see the situation for themselves. Those mice went, and they witnessed the cats sitting quietly with peaceful demeanor. They were all wearing prayer shawls, and they each had a string of prayer beads in their paws. They seemed very changed. The cats welcomed the mice warmly and spoke sweetly to them, showing them their hospitality. The delegation of mice returned home to give their report to their friends.

The mice at home were very excited to hear what the cats were like. The delegation said, "The cats have really changed. They're sitting peacefully, wearing prayer shawls, and they are all very religious now. They welcomed us and made us feel at home. There is only one problem."

"What's that?" asked the other mice.

"It's this," said the mice that went to investigate. "Their eyes still watch us in the same way as before."

PLAY WITH THIS STORY

Make cats' eyes. Cut out black cats' eyes and paste yellow pupils on them. Cover your paper with cats' eyes.

Play cat and mouse. All cats sit looking straight ahead. They cannot move their eyes from left to right. You can cover the cats' heads with scarves to limit their vision. If a cat is seen moving its eyes, it is disqualified from the game. Mice tiptoe one by one past the cats. The cats cannot move their eyes, but as soon as a cat sees a mouse, it can call out, "Meow!" The mouse has to freeze. When all mice are frozen, change roles.

Tell the truth. The cats were not telling the truth, but how could you tell? Have the children take turns telling a brief tale about something, adding in untrue parts. Listeners hold up one finger if they think they are hearing the truth. Two fingers if it sounds false to them.

Learn about the pilgrimage to Mecca. You might share *Going to Mecca* by Na'ima B. Robert and Valentina Cavallini. New York: Frances Lincoln Children's Books, 2014.

ABOUT THIS STORY

Collected in February 2006 from Cheto Ozel, Colemêrg (Hakkari) region, a speaker of both Kurmancî and English. The last phrase of this is used as a figure of speech. When troublemakers or brutal states don't act peacefully as they have promised, a saying from this story is used to describe them: "Their eyes are the same as before," "*Cawên wan yên berê ne*," meaning that their violent ways and games have not really changed.

SHENGAY AND PENGAY

*H*ebû tûnebû! There was and there was not a family of sheep. Every summer, when the weather became hot, the shepherd would take his sheep to the rich pasturelands high up in the mountains, the highlands called *zozan* (zoh-zahn). One year, one of the ewes had newborn lambs that were too young to travel, so they all stayed behind. The ewe named one of her lambs Shengay and the other Pengay.

As summer went on, the good grass in the lowlands was all gone, and the mother had to travel higher up for better food. She said to her children,

> "My Shengay, my Pengay!
> The grass on the lowlands is done,
> So up to zozan I run,
> Till back from grazing I come,
> Please open the door to no one."

The mother traveled far for food. When she returned, she stood outside the door and said,

> "My Shengay, my Pengay!
> My journey to zozan is done,
> I grazed on the grasses each one,
> The milk to my udders has come,
> Please open the door to your mom."

As the mother was saying these words, a wolf was listening near the door. He saw that when the two little lambs heard their mother's voice, they happily opened the door. The next day, their mother left for *zozan* again, and the wolf approached the door saying,

> "My Shengay, my Pengay!
> My journey to zozan is done,
> I grazed on the grasses each one,
> The milk to my udders has come,
> Now open the door to your mom."

The babies said, "No! You don't sound like our mother. We won't open the door."
"What does your mother's voice sound like?" asked the wolf.

Shengay and Pengay said, "Our mother's voice is clear, and her legs are white. Your voice is rough, and your legs are dark. You are a wolf, and you will come and eat us."

The wolf hid himself nearby until the mother came back. The mother came to the door and said,

> *"My Shengay, my Pengay!*
> *My journey to zozan is done,*
> *I grazed on the grasses each one,*
> *The milk to my udders has come,*
> *Please open the door to your mom."*

Shengay and Pengay opened the door. Both of them went to their mother and happily drank the milk. But the wolf outside the door had listened to how sweetly the ewe had spoken to her children, and he had seen how white her legs were. The next day, when the lambs' mother went to *zozan* again, the wolf covered his legs with flour, and clearing and sweetening his voice with honey, he called from outside the door,

> *"My Shengay, my Pengay!*
> *My journey to zozan is done,*
> *I grazed on the grasses each one,*
> *The milk to my udders has come,*
> *Now open the door to your mom."*

The lambs heard a sweet voice and saw legs that looked white, so they opened the door. When they opened the door, the bloodthirsty wolf rushed in and gobbled up Shengay. But Pengay hid, and though the wolf looked, he couldn't find her.

When the mother returned she saw that the door was open. She went inside, and there was the wolf sleeping on his back with his belly full and swollen. Little Pengay came out and told his mother what had happened to Shengay. The wolf was sleeping soundly, so while he slept they both dragged him down to the lake. There they cut his belly open, and little Shengay popped out as good as new. They filled the wolf's stomach with heavy stones and sewed it back up. The wolf woke up and stumbled over to the lake to get some water. He leaned over to drink and then he fell in and drowned from the weight of the stones. He never bothered little Shengay or little Pengay again.

> *If my story came out right,*
> *Now's the time to say goodnight.*

TELLING THIS STORY

Hebû tûnebû! This is pronounced heh-bu tu-neh-bu; the accent is on the first syllable of each word. This is a traditional Kurdish beginning of a folktale, meaning "there was and there was not."

PLAY WITH THIS STORY

Act it out. This story is fun to act out. Let the "wolves" tryout to see who can sing most like the mother. You can have many little goats. Perhaps each would like to make up its own name to rhyme with Pengay and Shengay.

Share Similar Stories

Lon Po Po: A Red Riding Hood Story from China by Ed Young (Puffin, 1996).
The Wolf and the Seven Little Kids by Ann Blades (Groundwood, 1999).
The Wolf and the Seven Kids by Brothers Grimm, illustrated by Keiko Kaichi (Hong Kong: minedition, 2014).
"Nsangi" in *Songs and Stories from Uganda* by W. Moses Serawadda and Hewit Pantaleoni, illustrated by Leo and Diane Dillon (Crowell, 1974). A gorilla swallows a little girl!

ABOUT THIS STORY

This story was collected in May 2006 from a 46-year-old woman in the Mardin region, Kurmancî. It was translated by Cheto Ozel.

This is Motif K311.3 *Thief disguises voice and is allowed access to goods (children).*

The best-known version of this tale is the Grimm's story *The Wolf and the Seven Little Kids.* MacDonald lists African American variants as well as variants from Germany, Spain, Africa, Tanganyika (Kamba), Jamaica, Taiwan, Korea, Uganda, and Haiti. MacDonald and Sturm include African American variants as well as variants from China, Benin, Germany, Russia, The Netherlands, France, and Indonesia.

For a collection of 34 variants of this tale, see *A Knock at the Door (The Oryx Multicultural Folktales Series)* by George Shannon (Phoenix: Oryx, 1992).

ABOUT THE AUTHOR

DIANE EDGECOMB is a professional storyteller who became involved with Kurdish refugees in the United States in 1999. After collecting stories from the refugees, Diane initiated The Kurdish Story Collection Project. She received grants to visit Kurdish villages in Turkey to collect folktales. From her collection of over 150 Kurdish tales, she selected those for her book *A Fire in My Heart: Kurdish Tales.*

Diane's Web site is http://livingmyth.com.

LAOS

From *Lao Folktales* by Wajuppa Tossa with Kongdeuan Nettavong. Edited by Margaret Read MacDonald (Libraries Unlimited, 2008).

A FLYING LESSON

Retold by Phra Sunantha Theerapanyo Phikkhu.

Once the Buddha was born King of the Vultures. He was so well revered and respected by all for his loving kindness, compassion, generosity, and devotion to his subjects and his own family. When he became a father, he was one of the best fathers. He brought up his son with love and warmth. When it was time for his son to learn to fly, he and his wife would teach the son to fly.

The first lesson was to fly from the nest to the ground. The king was proud to have such a strong and able son who could fly beautifully in his first lesson. Then the flying lesson would get higher and higher each day. They taught the son until he was strong enough to practice flying without the parents' supervision.

Each day, they would ask the son, "How high did you fly today, my son?"

"Oh, today I flew up to the top of the tallest tree in the forest, Father and Mother," came the answer from the son.

"Be careful to observe what you can see down below, my son," his mother would say.

"When the rice field seems as small as a human palm, the house as small as a buffalo dung pile, and the river as narrow as a human arm, you must not fly any higher," said his father.

"Yes, Father, Mother; I have not reached that height yet," said the son.

The next day, the son went out flying again. When he returned, his parents asked him again.

"How high did you fly today, my son?"

"Oh, Father, Mother, today I flew up high, but I have not reached that height that you mentioned yet," answered the son.

"Be careful to observe what you can see down below, my son," his mother would say.

"Remember when you see the rice field as small as a human palm, the house as small as a buffalo dung pile, and the river as narrow as a human arm, you must not fly any higher," said his father.

"Yes, Father, Mother; I haven't gone up that high yet," said the son again.

The next day, the son went out flying again.

He flew up higher and higher. He flew up so high, yet he was still not tired. He kept taking a higher and higher flight. Then he thought, "I should look down now to see if I can see the small rice field, the small house, and the narrow river."

The young vulture looked down. And lo and behold, the rice field was as small as a human palm, the house as small as a buffalo dung pile, and the river as narrow as a human arm.

"Yes! I did it. I can see the small rice field, the small house, and the narrow river. I have flown the highest flight any bird can." He was so happy and proud of what he could do.

"How wonderful it is that I could do it! Yet I am still not feeling tired at all. Perhaps, my parents' warning was for some older birds," he thought.

"I could fly higher, for I am still young and strong," he told himself.

So, he flew up and up and up and up. . . .

All of a sudden, he felt his wings were fluttering, his body swaying here and there, his eyes growing dim. He then realized that in the higher atmosphere, strong winds came from every direction and it was impossible to maintain his equilibrium.

That was the last thing he remembered. His body was hurled down fast, and faster, and faster. All he could remember was his own calling, "Father, Mother, help."

Back at his nest, the parents were waiting for their beloved son to return. They had no chance of asking how high he flew that day . . . or the next.

The young vulture woke up again hanging on a branch of a tall tree far away from his own nest.

"Now I know what my parents meant by telling me not to fly too high. I should have stopped when the rice field looked as small as a human palm, the house as small as a buffalo dung pile, and the river as narrow as a human arm. They warned me. But I did not listen."

That was the lesson the young vulture learned. He promised himself that he would remember the lesson he had learned and teach it to his own children in the future . . . the "Flying Lesson."

PLAY WITH THIS STORY

Compare with the Greek myth of Icarus. Icarus makes wings of wax and flies too close to the sun. You can find his story in most collections of Greek mythology. *Mythology* by Edith Hamilton (Little, Brown, Co., 2012) is a good, comprehensive collection.

Fly. Provide large sheets of paper for the children to cut out large paper wings and decorate. Fasten the wings to their arms and retell the story as the children fly higher and higher. In some versions of this story, the flyer looks down and sees things looking smaller and smaller. First, a lake looks like a pond, then a puddle, then a teacup. Discuss how the hill would look as the flyer went up and up. The river? The rice field? You could have the young bird fly back home after each flight and tell his parents how things looked. Okay so far. Then he flies higher. Still okay. Then he reaches the height his parents had warned him about.

ABOUT THIS STORY

This tale was told to Wajuppa Tossa by the Buddhist monk Phra Sunantha Theerapanyo Phikkhu. This is Motif K1041 *Borrowed feathers*. This motif is one of the oldest stories ever recorded. A 4,000-year-old precursor to this story appears in *The Oldest Stories in the World* by Theodor H. Gaster (Boston: Beacon Press, 1958).

THE SERVING GIANT

Told by Pha Sunantha Theerapanyo Phikkhu, Vientiane, Laos. English Retelling by Wajuppa Tossa.

Once there was a farmer who worked very hard but he remained poor. One day he was digging the ground to clear the field for the approaching planting season. As he was digging, his hoe hit hard on an object. It was an earthen jar.

"Oh, I am going to be rich. It must be a pot of silver and gold as in the old folktales," thought the farmer.

He hurriedly opened the jar.

Once the jar was opened, smoke came out of the jar. The farmer became so frightened. He had never heard of smoke coming out of any jar before. His knees dropped, and he was sitting there waiting to see what would happen.

The smoke began to form, and in a short time there was a huge giant right in front of the farmer.

The man was so frightened that he put his palms together, ready to beg for his life. But, the giant bent down to say, "Oh, my dear master, please don't be afraid of me. I am your servant. I am ready to serve you with whatever you order me to do. Please give me orders now. There is one condition, . . . you must find work for me to do nonstop. Whenever you have nothing more for me to do, I will eat you up."

The farmer was so frightened that he had to think fast to save his life.

"How about if you build me a fully furnished house complete with a beautiful garden?" asked the farmer, thinking that it would take a long time for the giant to pull out the old house and get wood and begin to build the house. Thus, he would feel safe for quite a while.

"Oh, yes, Master, I am at your service right away," said the giant.

But it did not take him more than a few minutes to complete this first order. The giant just put his palms together and recited words of incantation, "*Ohm phiang. . . .*"

And there was a beautiful, large wooden house fully furnished with furniture, bedding, kitchen utensils, and everything. Outside there was a splendid flower, vegetable, and herb garden.

"Master, what else do you want me to do?" asked the giant.

Now the farmer had to think quickly. "How about a fruit orchard and rice fields together with a stream running through the land?" asked the farmer. Again the farmer thought it would surely take the giant a long time to dig up the ground and plant the fruit trees and rice seedlings. But . . . it did not take the giant more than a few minutes to complete the second order.

The giant just put his palms together and recited words of incantation, "*Ohm phiang. . . .*" All of a sudden, a beautiful fruit orchard and rice fields were there near his land. There was even a stream with clear running water that ran alongside the fruit orchard and the rice fields.

"Master, what else do you want me to do? Remember if you stop telling me to do work, I will eat you up," said the giant.

"How about finding servants to take care of the house and the garden? And workers to work in the orchard and the rice fields?" ordered the farmer. Again the farmer thought it would surely take the giant a long time to find all the people to do housework and fieldwork. But . . . it did not take the giant more than a few minutes to complete the third order.

The giant just put his palms together and recited words of incantation, "*Ohm phiang. . . .*" All of a sudden, his house was full of servants and his orchard and rice fields were full of workers, working away diligently.

"Master, what else do you want me to do? Remember if you stop telling me to do work, I will eat you up," said the giant.

And so the farmer kept ordering the giant to do work nonstop for him. He was still safe as long as he was awake and could give orders. However, as the sun was going down, the farmer became more worried. It would be bedtime very soon as the sun had just gone down. During the daytime, the farmer was not so worried. He could always ask the giant to do this and that, but what would happen during the night? He would not be able to give orders for the giant to do any work. And that's when the giant would eat him up.

"Master, what else do you want me to do? Remember if you stop telling me to do work, I will eat you up," said the giant.

What else could he ask the giant to do while he was sleeping? After a long time, the farmer had an idea. He ordered the giant to do one endless job. With that order, he was able to go to sleep restfully. The giant began that job early in the evening of that day. When the farmer woke up, the giant was still working at it. For all I know, the giant may have still been doing that job. And the farmer lived happily ever after.

Here is the riddle: "What kind of job did the farmer order the giant to do to make him work nonstop?"

Here is the answer given by Pha Wiangsamai of Vientiane in his telling of this story: The farmer said, "Now, I would like you to build a round pillar of 40 meters tall right in front of my house. Then, you must climb up to the top of the pillar. Once you are at the top, you must climb down. Keep climbing up and down until I give you a new order."

PLAY WITH THIS STORY

Make an answer list. Many answers are possible. Here are some answers that were given to Dr. Wajuppa Tossa when she told this story to audiences: One child suggested telling the giant to guard the house and property. Another said to ask the giant to travel throughout the entire universe (which is endless as far as we know). Someone had heard similar giant tales before and suggested the traditional folk motif of asking the giant to show how it could fit into such a small jar and then putting the top back onto the jar. One of the monks in Vientiane said, "The farmer ordered the giant to study because studying would be endless." And one bright child suggested simply that the giant be told to go to sleep and not wake up!

Let the children suggest their own answers. You could make an answer list by posting their answers on a long ribbon. Let them keep adding more answers on succeeding days as they think of them. Any endless task is a correct answer to this riddle.

ABOUT THIS STORY

This riddle tale was told to Wajuppa Tossa by Pha Suanantha Theereapanyo Phikku, a Buddhist monk in Vientiane, Laos. It includes motifs N813 *Helpful genie* and K211 *Devil cheated by imposing an impossible task*.

ABOUT THE STORYTELLER

DR. WAJUPPA TOSSA, of Mahasarakham University, retold these stories. Wajuppa grew up in the small town of Tat Phanom, on the banks of the Mekong River. Her Thai home was right across the river from Laos. Northeastern Thailand (Isaan) is Lao speaking and culturally Lao. But in recent years, the Bangkok Thai culture and language have overtaken this region, and the local Lao traditions are being lost. Dr. Wajuppa strives to renew interest in her Lao heritage by teaching teachers to tell local folktales and encouraging them to share these stories in the Lao language.

Dr. Wajuppa continues to collect stories from tellers in villages in Isaan (Northeastern Thailand) and across the river in Laos. Her friend Kong-deuane Nettavong, Director of the Lao National Library in Vientiane, has assisted her with this work.

To encourage storytelling in Isaan, Dr. Wajuppa holds an annual storytelling festival, inviting tellers from other Southeast Asian countries to come share their tales in Thailand. And she and her students travel to schools throughout Isaan every year telling stories and encouraging teachers to begin sharing tales with their children. Photo of Dr. Wajuppa Tossa, left, and Kongdeuane Nettavong.

ABOUT THE EDITOR

Dr. Margaret Read MacDonald was invited by Dr. Wajuppa as a Fulbright Scholar to work with her at Mahasarakham University in 1995 and 1996. Since then they have collaborated on numerous articles, books and storytelling projects both in Thailand and in the United States.

MALAYSIA

From *The Singing Top: Tales from Malaysia, Singapore, and Brunei* by Margaret Read MacDonald (Libraries Unlimited, 2008).

SUMANDAK AND THE ORANGUTAN

A Kadazandusun Folktale. As told by Yunis Rojiin Gabu, heard from her grandmother, Gunih Rampasan of Kampong Togop Tamparuli, Sabah. Copyright Yunis Rojin 2006.

One day Sumandak was in her garden working.

Suddenly a HUGE Orangutan leapt out of the jungle, grabbed Sumandak, and carried her off. Though she kicked and screamed, she could not break loose. The Orangutan carried her deep into the jungle and up a tall tree. There he kept her in his tree. She could not get down from this tall perch. There were no long vines that she could hang on to, no way to climb down.

But the Orangutan did not hurt Sumandak. In fact, he was in love with her!

"You are SO beautiful," said the Orangutan. "You will be very happy here as my wife. In seven days my relatives will come, and we will have the wedding."

"How can I marry an Orangutan?" thought Sumandak. "But how can I get down from here? This tree is too tall. If I jump, I will die. It is hopeless." She could see that there were no vines at all near the top of the tree, nothing to hold on to, to lower herself to the ground.

The next day the Orangutan brought her food. She ate it. But she kept the skins and did not throw them out.

The Orangutan was very messy. There were vines and twigs sticking into his hair all over. Suddenly the girl had an idea! If she could pull out some of the Orangutan's long hair, perhaps she could weave a rope!

"Dear Orangutan, you are SO messy. Let me help you clean yourself up."

"Am I messy? I didn't know that." The Orangutan felt very embarrassed. He wanted to make a good impression on Sumandak. He was bringing her the best fruits every night. He really wanted her to like him.

"I can help. Just sit down here, and I will take away all those vines and twigs sticking out."

So the Orangutan sat quietly, and Sumandak began to groom him. Slowly she combed his hair. And she put aside all of the twigs and vines she removed. She did not throw anything away.

The Orangutan soon fell fast asleep as she combed his fur. When he was sleeping deeply, Sumandak pulled out a handful of fur.

"Ouch! What was that?"

"Dear Orangutan, did you feel that? I was just tickling you a bit."

"OK." The Orangutan went back to sleep.

Next day Sumandak did the same thing.

"Come sit here, dear Orangutan. I will clean you up a bit."

And when he was sleeping . . .

"Ouch! What was that?"

"Oh, silly Orangutan. Don't you like it when I tickle you a little?"

And so, day by day, Sumandak was able to save quite a pile of Orangutan fur. And while he slept, she began to weave a rope, which she hid from the Orangutan.

By the third day she had a long rope. When the Orangutan was gone out foraging for food, she lowered the rope from the treetop. It was not long enough.

But the fourth day the rope was getting longer. But when she tested it, it was not long enough yet.

On the fifth day, when the Orangutan came home in the evening, he said, "I think I am handsome enough now. You won't need to clean my fur anymore. Look how good I look. And my fur is feeling very light. I don't want you to pull on it anymore."

"Your face could still use a little help," said the girl. "I think if I trimmed your hairy face a bit you would look more handsome yet."

"Well, alright." And the Orangutan let her trim his face.

So by the sixth day the rope was very long. As soon as the Orangutan left the tree, the girl dropped the rope and prepared to climb down, but it was still not long enough. The situation was becoming drastic. On the seventh day the Orangutan's relatives would arrive for the wedding. If she didn't escape before then it would be too late.

That night when the Orangutan arrived home, he was very excited. "Tomorrow is our wedding, girl! My relatives will come, and you will become my bride!"

"Then I must clean you up some more," said Sumandak.

"No, I don't think so. I am already handsome enough," said the Orangutan. "Besides if you trim anymore of my hair, I will be too chilly."

"You do look handsome now," said Sumandak. "But you know we forgot to trim your tail. I think I should just trim a bit there."

So the Orangutan let her trim some hair from his tail.

After a while the Orangutan fell asleep. Sumandak could see that she needed just a little more hair to finish her rope. So she began to pull really hard at the last hairs on his tail.

"What are you doing?"

"Oh dear Orangutan, there is a bad stain here. I have to scrub really hard to get it out. You want to look so beautiful tomorrow when your family comes. Just let me finish cleaning you up."

The Oranguatan thought she was really trying to make him beautiful. He did not suspect one thing. So he fell back asleep.

Quietly the girl lowered the rope from the treetop. Down and down it went . . . far below. She could see that the rope was long enough!

Quickly she climbed down the rope and ran away home through the forest.

In the morning, the Orangutan woke up. "Today is my wedding day! My relatives will come soon!"

But alas . . . Sumandak was gone. He had been tricked!

TELLING THIS TALE

When Yunis Rojiin Gabu told this story, she said, "I didn't like the ending . . . because Grandma said just, 'He had been tricked!' There was no more elaboration. But it got me thinking." Perhaps you can make up your own ending to the story. What did the Orangutan do, now that his human bride had escaped? I like to add an ending in which the relatives arrive for the wedding, and there is a lovely young Orangutan girl among them. Our Orangutan falls instantly in love, and there is a wedding for him after all.

PLAY WITH THIS STORY

Make a rope. For younger children, give each child a large piece of paper with a tree drawn on it. Provide leaves, vines, and grasses and let them create a rope from the tree to the ground by pasting the objects in a line leading from tree to ground. For older children, provide a pile of leaves, twigs, vines, and long grasses. Let the children weave ropes using these materials. How long can they make them?

Compare to Similar Stories

Share and compare other picture books about animal husbands:

The Great Smelly, Slobbery, Small-Tooth Dog by Margaret Read MacDonald (August House, 2007).

Beauty and the Beast by Marianne Mercer (New York: Four Winds, 1978).

Snowbear Whittington: An Appalachian Beauty and the Beast by William H. Hooks (New York: MacMillan, 1994).

ABOUT THIS STORY

This story has similarities with Type 425C *Beauty and the Beast* (D735.1). However, in the orangutan story, the girl does *not* marry the beast. Instead, the tale becomes G530 *Escape from ogre.* The story was collected from Yunis Rojiin Gabu of Kota Kinabalu, Sabah. Yunis heard the story from her grandmother, Gunih Rampasan.

A Note from the Author

This was told to me at the Sabah State Library in Kota Kinabalu in August 2006 during a break in our storytelling workshop. Yunis had been thinking about stories from her grandmother that she could tell me. She had shared "Rolling Red-eyed Head" and "Terrible Karamboa" with my daughter and son-in-law and myself during our 2003 storytelling tour, and I had typed them up and given Yunis copies. She knew that I would like to hear more stories, so she emailed me and said, "Bring your tape recorder!" She had a headful of tales ready to share with me when I visited again.

THE SINGING TOP
A Story from Perak

In some parts of Malaysia, young men love to play a game called gasing. *This is played with a large wooden top. The men wrap a cord tightly around the top and then throw it hard at a certain spot on the ground. If thrown well, the top will spin steadily in that spot for a very long time. Some say that good top players have thrown tops that would spin for two hours or more.*

In Kampung Mengkudu Kuning, there once lived a young man who was exceptional at playing *gasing*. When he threw his top, it would spin and spin, often much longer than the other players. He took special care of his top. And when he spun it, it seemed that it actually spoke. It seemed that it sang, "*Mengkudu kuning . . . mengkudu kuning . . . mengkudu kuning. . . .*" This was the name of the village. The village was named for the yellow *mengkudu* fruit, because so many of these delicious fruited trees grew around the village. So the top could also be thought to be singing, "Yellow mengkudu . . . yellow mengkudu . . . yellow mengkudu. . . ." It was maybe singing about the delicious yellow fruit.

Now the Raja heard of this amazing singing top. So he sent for the young man to be brought to the palace. "Let me hear your top sing!" commanded the Raja.

The young man threw the top. "*Mengkudu kuning . . . mengkudu kuning . . .,*" sang the top. And then it began to talk! "Jungle . . . jungle . . . tree . . . tree . . . *puteri . . . puteri. . . .*"

Puteri means princess. The Raja bent to listen more closely. And suddenly the top began to chant a *pantun*—a poem!

> *Nyior manis tepi pengkalan,*
> *Tempat merak bersarang tujoh.*
> *Hitam manis turun berjalan,*
> *Bagai kilat bintang sa-puloh.*

> There's a sweet coconut at the jetty's edge,
> Where the seven peacock's nest.
> My dark girl comes out to walk,
> As bright as ten stars shining.

The raja was entranced. "Go at once!" he ordered. "Take your talking top, and find this beautiful princess. Bring her to me. She will be a bride for my son!"

The young man was in trouble now. How could he find a princess in some far-off jungle? He left the palace and started through the forest. But it seemed hopeless. At last he stopped to rest. He took his top out, looked at it, and threw it. As soon as the top began to spin, it started to speak again. "Follow the path . . . a coconut grove . . . tallest tree . . . that is the place. . . ."

So he set out again. And after a long time traveling along the path, sure enough, there was a coconut grove. And in the middle of the grove was a tall, tall tree.

A sweet feminine voice sang down from the treetop,

> *Chinchin permata batu-nya retak,*
> *Pakaian anak Raja Muda,*
> *Musim durian rambutan masak,*
> *Manggis menumpang bertarok muda.*

> A ring with a cracked gem.
> Worn by the prince's son.
> Durian's in season, the rambutan's ripe,
> While the mangosteen's only green as yet.

The young man laughed. The *pantun* poem meant, "You can't have everything at once." He replied in verse,

> From Pulau Indera Sakti
> I come to ask one thing.
> The Rajah sends me here
> to bring his son a bride.

There was laughter from the treetop. Then a ladder was lowered down the tree, and a beautiful young maiden lightly descended.

"I am glad to see you come for me. My father has said that the one I should marry would come. I am Puteri Kelapa Gading. I say, welcome my husband to be!"

"No! You misunderstand. I come to take you as bride for the Raja's son."

But Puteri Kelapa Gading simply smiled and shook her head.

"My father has said, 'The one who comes to find you, that is the one you will marry.'"

What a predicament. Of course he couldn't help falling in love with this beautiful creature. But what to do?

He picked up his top and spun it.

Round and round whirled the top. And it seemed to say, "Honesty . . . trust . . . honesty . . . trust. . . ."

So he brought the beautiful Puteri Kelapa Gading back to the Raja's court. He confessed to the Raja all that had happened.

The Raja was furious. This girl was to be the bride of his own son, not that of some village boy. But fortunately there was a wise man in the Raja's court. He could see that Puteri Kelapa Gading, Princess Yellow Coconut, was no ordinary girl. She came from the special yellow coconut tree. Her name, *Kelapa Gading*, meant "yellow coconut." And it was clear that she wanted to marry the young man from the village of the yellow *mengkudu* fruit.

"It might be dangerous to our land to deny this woman her choice of husband," advised the elder. "I suspect she is of magical ancestry."

So the Raja acceded. "Very well, I will find another bride for my son."

The Raja announced to all, "The princess Puteri Kalapa Gading has chosen a husband. She will marry the brave young man from the village of Mengkudu Kuning!"

And so it was.

They say that whenever the young man threw his top after that, it hummed only one thing, "*Mengkudu kuning . . . mengkugu kuning . . . mengkudu kuning. . . .*" But sometimes, if he threw the top very, very hard, it would seem to jump for joy and would hum, "*Kalapa gading . . . kalapa gading . . . kalapa gading. . . .*"

TELLING THIS STORY

Make the chanting of "*mengkudu kuning*" and "*kalapa gading*" sound like a rolling, spinning top. Repeat the phrases several times in a rhythm, letting the "ing" ring out. Because the top was said to speak *pantun*, I inserted Malaysian *pantun* (poems) into the story. You can leave those out if they prove too cumbersome for you.

PLAY WITH THIS STORY

Spin a top. Bring in a few high-quality, well-balanced tops and let the children take turns seeing how long they can make each spin.

Make a toy top. One easy pattern requires only milk carton bottle caps and a toothpick. You need to first pierce a hole in the lid with a nail and hammer. Let the children insert the toothpick and begin to spin! (http://www.youtube.com/watch?v=ue5zd0ef3T4)

Watch Malaysians demonstrate *gasing*. You can watch teens show how to play children's *gasing* on YouTube (http://www.youtube.com/watch?v=liC2vt9FLzw). *Gasing* is played by adult men in Malaysian villages. Competitions are held to see whose top can spin the longest. Some spin two hours or longer. They are thrown, caught up, and set in special holders to spin. See a top maker show how to spin the adult player's top: http://www.youtube.com/watch?v=LU9z48ulYf8.

ABOUT THIS STORY

This folktale is from the Malaysian state of Perak. This is Motif T75.3 *Unrequited love expressed in song (poem)* and Motif T11.1.1 *Beauty of woman reported to king causes quest for her as bride.*

Pulau Indera Sakti is the island on which the first sultan of Perak set foot when he came from Malacca. Each new sultan must dip his foot in the water there when he is installed. The Malay *pantun* is a poetic form that was often used in courtship. The boy and girl would chant enigmatic or riddle poems back and forth to each other.

ABOUT THE AUTHOR

MARGARET READ MACDONALD frequently visits Malaysia and Singapore to tell stories and has heard many tales from tellers while she was there. She was especially excited to hear stories from Yunis Rojiin Gabu while she was visiting the Malaysian state of Sabah on the island of Borneo. Yunis was the Sabah State Library representative in charge of Margaret's storytelling tour. One day, when they were returning in a van, along with Margaret's daughter, Jen Whitman, and her husband, Nat (who were also telling stories that day), Yunis suddenly said, "Your stories remind me of stories my grandmother told."

Yunis began to tell the most amazing stories. Margaret quickly began to write them down, and Nat grabbed pencil and paper and jotted down the tunes for the songs in the stories. The next time Margaret came to do workshops in Sabah, Yunis was ready with many more stories she had remembered. These tales had never been written down and were preserved only because of that one moment when Yunis suddenly remembered.

Margaret Read MacDonald was a Children's Librarian with the King County Library System, has a PhD in Folklore from Indiana University, and now travels the world telling stories. She has written over 65 books on folklore and storytelling topics, including *Teaching with Story: Classroom Connections to Storytelling*, coauthored by Jen and Nat Whitman (August House, 2013).

MEXICO

From *The Eagle on the Cactus: Traditional Stories from Mexico. El águila encima del nopal: Cuentos tradicionales de México.* Retold by Angel Vigil (Libraries Unlimited, 2000). For a Spanish version of this story, see *The Eagle on the Cactus*, pp. 201–202.

THE OWL AND THE PAINTED BIRD

A long time ago, during the time when the world was new, animals across the earth were busy developing their natures and appearances. The birds of the world were especially active at this time.

Each bird was learning the songs that would be their own and that would identify that particular bird to the other animals. They were also trying on feathers that would mark each type of bird as distinct and beautiful.

One bird, Pi-coo, was having an especially difficult time. She could not make up her mind about which feathers she should wear. The more she tried on, the more confused she became. Soon, almost all of the feathers were spoken for, and she was left with almost nothing to cover her naked body. Because she had no feathers, she was very ashamed and refused to come out of her nest. The other birds felt sorry for her. They gathered together and talked about a way they could help Pi-coo.

The eagle, who spoke first, said, "Why don't we each give her one feather? We all have so many. It wouldn't be missed and would really help her."

The other birds were not so sure about the idea, but not one bird could come up with another plan. The birds worried that if they each gave a feather to Pi-coo, she might become the most beautiful of all the birds.

Finally, the wise old owl spoke up. He said, "Why don't we each just loan her a feather? Then she will be covered. As soon as her own feathers grow in, then she will return our feathers. I myself will be responsible for the return of the feathers."

The other birds agreed to this plan only because of the guarantee by the wise old owl to return their feathers.

Soon all the birds had given Pi-coo a feather. She gathered all of the feathers and carefully arranged them on her naked body. As soon as she saw her reflection in the still waters of the river, she realized that she was the most beautiful of all the birds. She looked like a

---

painted bird, with all the colors of the rainbow shining on her magnificent body. Realizing that the other birds would be jealous and would never allow her to keep their feathers, she immediately flew high into the sky, never to return.

It was not long before the birds realized that Pi-coo was not returning. Incensed, they searched for the wise old owl, but he was nowhere to be found. They could not stand the idea that Pi-coo was now the most beautiful of the birds and demanded that the wise old owl keep his word and return the donated feathers.

The wise old owl knew how angry the other birds were. So he hid in the trees during the day and came out only at night when he knew that the other birds were sleeping. During the night, he would quietly fly around and call out for Pi-coo, "Pi-coo. Pi-coo."

And that is why, to this day, the owl is a nocturnal bird, only coming out at night to fly through the air with its plaintive, searching cry of "Pi-coo. Pi-coo."

PLAY WITH THIS STORY

Make a feathered bird picture. Give each child a cutout of a large bird (or a drawing of a large bird). Provide multicolored paper feathers, or real feathers from a craft shop, to paste on the bird. If you are studying bird species, you might photocopy pictures of feathers of various birds and provide those to paste on.

Act it out. Assign bird parts and let each child select a bird feather to tape onto the child playing the pi-coo. Let the pi-coo wear a plain brown shirt or coat to which the children can affix their feathers. Pi-coo flies away out of sight, but pokes his head out and calls back, "Pi-coo! Pi-coo!" at the tale's end.

ABOUT THIS STORY

Motif A2313.8* *Origin of owl's feathers. Owl lent feathers by other birds for ball. He never returns.*

A Puerto Rican version of this story is found in *The Acorn Tree and Other Folktales* by Anne Rockwell (New York: Greenwillow, 1995), pp. 20–22, and in *Three Wishes: A Collection of Puerto Rican Folktales* by Ricardo Alegría (New York: Harcourt, Brace 7 World, 1969), pp. 64–75.

ABOUT THE AUTHOR

ANGEL VIGIL first heard his beloved stories while listening to his grandfather and Tio Joe, the family storytellers, in the northern villages of New Mexico. His most common childhood memories involve large family gatherings: birthday parties, weddings, baptisms, Easter, Christmas, church, picnics, and, yes, even funerals. A simple recitation of a few of his memories reveals a rich childhood life centered in family experience and strong in Hispanic heritage.

He remembers going to his grandmother's farm and eating a delicious white homemade goat cheese with a heavy sweet molasses poured on it. He heard his father singing an old, joyous Spanish song at a wedding. He tasted the fresh, warm, just-off-the-griddle, jam-covered tortillas his aunt made especially for him whenever he came for a visit. He felt the small, hard beans under his little fingers as he sorted them from one pile to another, carefully completing his childhood job of cleaning the beans by separating the rocks from the beans before they are cooked.

He saw his mother kneeling and praying, eyes closed, hands folded, before the altar to "*la Virgen*" she kept in her bedroom. He heard his mother sternly admonishing him not to turn around in church or he'd turn to stone. He heard the rustle of his sister's fancy, lacy white First Communion dress. He saw his parents, aunts, and uncles sitting around a large, round kitchen table at his grandfather's house on the farm, sharing a pot of *posole* with red chile, telling *cuentos*, laughing and reminiscing about the good old days, their own childhood. He heard the hushed, droning, muffled voices of his aunts saying the rosary at a *velorio*, or at a wake before a funeral. He felt his parents' warm and firm hands on his head as they gave him their blessing when he left home.

His childhood memories reveal a truth about his family—the realization that his own family was a living example of Hispanic centuries-old cultural traditions and a repository of generations of Hispanic culture. It was in this rich and deeply felt family life that Angel first heard his beloved stories.

Angel Vigil is Chairman of the Fine and Performing Arts Department and Director of Drama at Colorado Academy in Denver. He is an award-winning author, performer, stage director, and teacher. He has received the Heritage Artist Award and the Master Artist Award from the Colorado Council on the Arts.

Angel's Web site is www.angelvigil.com.

MONGOLIA

From *Mongolian Folktales*, retold by Dashdondog Jamba and Borolzoi Dashdondog. Edited by Anne Pellowski (Libraries Unlimited, 2009).

THE FOUR WISE MEN

Khar in *Mongolian is black,* shar *is yellow, and* tsagaan *is white. The suffixes in the names in this story indicate they represent black, yellow, and white persons. The Bayandai represent the Mongol people. This is a parable to indicate that the Mongolian people believe they were helped by persons of the different races to become the distinct people they are today.*

Once upon a time, in Mongolia, a wise man named Bayandai lived on a mountain. He had

thousands of horses on the northern side,
thousands of cows on the southern side,
thousands of sheep in the lower fields,
thousands of camels in the steppes, and
thousands of goats among the rocks on the top of the mountain.

One day a big monster appeared with

a head the size of a cauldron,
a stomach the size of a house,
arms five feet long, and
feet ten times bigger than any human.

The monster opened his mouth and said, "Do you like

your horses on your northern side,
your cows on your southern side,
your sheep in the fields,
your camels on the steppe,
your goats on the high rocks, or
do you like your life?"

Wise man Bayandai caressed his long beard. Then he answered straight out. "I like

my horses on the northern side,
my cows on the southern side,
my sheep in the field,
my camels in the steppe,
my goats among the rocks, and
I like my life! You may eat me, but only the steel knife of another wise man, Kharaadai, can cut me."

The big monster went to the other wise man, Kharaadai. "Give me your steel knife!" he threatened.

Kharaadai caressed his black beard and answered, "I will give you my steel knife, but it can only be brandished while riding the dun stallion that belongs to another wise man, Sharaadai."

The big monster went to Sharaadai and demanded, "Give me your dun stallion!"

The wise man Sharaadai caressed his yellow beard and said, "I will give you my dun stallion, but nothing can catch it except the lasso of Tsagaadai."

The monster went to Tsagaadai. "Give me your lasso," he ordered.

Wise man Tsagaadai caressed his white beard and said, "I would give you my lasso, but it is far away on the other side of the sea. It is very difficult, but I can tell you how to go there if you wish."

"Yes, tell me. How do I get to the other side of the sea?" asked the monster.

Wise man Tsagaadai caressed his beard again. Then he said, "First, you must find a large, round stone as big as your stomach, and a smaller one the size of your head. Then you must tie the big stone around your neck with a strong rope, and the smaller one around your legs with a shorter rope. You will need those to catch the lasso. Then you must jump into the sea and swim as fast as you can to the other side. There you will find the lasso."

The monster did as he was told. He tied a big stone around his neck and a smaller stone around his legs. He jumped into the sea. But he never came back with the lasso of Tsagaadai. He never captured the dun horse of Sharaadai. He never brandished the steel knife of Kharaadai. And he never came back to get Bayandai and his

thousands of horses on the northern side,
thousands of cows on the southern side,
thousands of sheep in the fields,
thousands of camels in the steppe, and
thousands of goats among the rocks on the top of the mountain.

PLAY WITH THIS STORY

Make three beards. Make a photocopy of a picture showing three identical yurts. Have the children draw a stick figure beside each yurt. Then paste yarn beards of black, yellow, and white onto their stick figures.

ABOUT THIS STORY

Motif A531 *Culture hero overcomes a monster.*

This is an unusual story with its directional chants and its colored beards. The motif of sending someone on another and another wild goose chase, though, is common in folklore.

THE GOATS, THE KIDS, AND THE WOLVES

This drawing story is remarkably similar to one that was common in North America in the 19th century. Where it truly originated is hard to tell. When telling this, if possible, use chalk on a blackboard or a marker on white board. If using marker on paper, disregard the instructions about erasing.

Once upon a time, there lived an old man and a woman. Like most people in Mongolia, they lived in a round home called a *ger*. [Draw a circle.]

In the middle of the top of the *ger* was a round opening, to let in the sunshine and let out the smoke. [Add a small circle inside the first circle.]

Near their *ger* was a fenced-in pen in which they kept their five black goats and three baby kids. [Draw an oval with five larger dots and three smaller ones.]

Not too far from this pen were two bushes. Hidden behind these bushes, two wolves had their den. If you walked by at night, you could see only their eyes, shining in the darkness. [Draw two small semicircles below the oval, with two dots in each.]

One morning the old man went down to the pen to get the three little kids. He brought them back to the *ger* and tethered them on ropes attached to the back of the *ger*. There they could eat the fresh new grass. [Erase three small dots, draw a line from the oval to the circle, and place three small dots at the ends of three lines on top of the circle.]

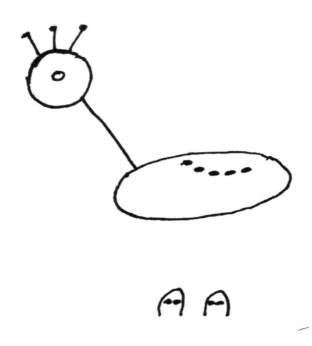

The old man then went outside to have a good look around. When he saw no sign of danger, he went back to the *ger*. [Draw a beak on the right side of the circle. Draw one line to each semicircle.]

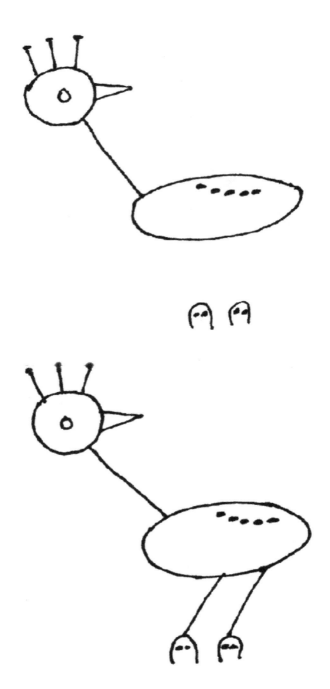

The moment the wolves saw that the man had gone back inside the *ger*, they ran to the pen and jumped over the fence. The five goats inside were so frightened, they jumped over the back part of the fence. Each goat went in a different direction, bleating loudly. [Erase five dots inside the oval and redraw them, with lines, at the back of the oval.]

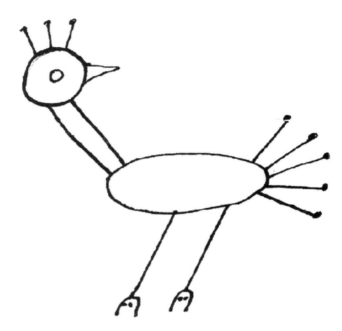

The old woman heard the commotion and came out of the *ger*. She ran to the pen. "Oh, where are our goats?" she cried. "All I see is a strange bird!"

TELLING THIS STORY

Practice drawing this story as you tell it several times to be sure you can create the desired effect at the end.

PLAY WITH THIS STORY

Draw the story. After telling the story and demonstrating it again, pass out pencil and paper and lead the children through telling and drawing the tale.

ABOUT THIS STORY

Anne Pellowski developed this version from an oral version by German children's book author Fritz Muhlenweg, who spent time in Mongolia and wrote the book *Big Tiger and Christian* (New York:

Pantheon, 1952). Two versions also appear in *Mongolische Volksmärchen* by Walter Heissig (Dusseldorf: F. Diedrichs, 1963).

Share Similar Stories

"Turkey Tale" in *Twenty Tellable Tales* by Margaret Read MacDonald (New York: H.W. Wilson, 1986), pp. 90–94
On the Banks of Plum Creek by Laura Ingalls Wilder (New York: HarperCollins, 1953), p. 318.

ABOUT THE AUTHORS

DASHDONDOG JAMBA is one of the leading children's book authors of Mongolia. Dashdondog founded the Mongolian Children's Mobile Library.

ANNE PELLOWSKI was employed by the U.S. Fund for UNICEF from 1966 to 1981 as the founding director of the Information Center on Children's Cultures. After leaving this position, she divided her time between writing and traveling throughout the world as a consultant to UNICEF, UNESCO, the World Council of Churches, and many other international organizations. Late in her eighth decade of life, Anne Pellowski continues to travel the world giving presentations on storytelling and empowering her listeners to tell their own stories in locales such as Ethiopia and Honduras. She also volunteers her time to establish children's libraries in underprivileged nations; most recently she led a parish mission to Nicaragua for this purpose in February 2013.

NEPAL

From *From the Mango Tree and Other Folktales from Nepal* by Kavita Ram Shrestha and Sarah Lamstein (Libraries Unlimited, 1997).

THE CAVE OF HALESI

Caves, like the rivers in Nepal, are considered sacred, for they were places of meditation for the saints, or holy men. The Cave of Halesi is a place of religious pilgrimages.

Long ago, the demon Bhasmasur worshipped *Lord Mahadeva*, god of destruction. Lord Mahadeva was so pleased by the demon's worship that he appeared before him, saying, "What is it you want? Tell me, so I may fulfill your wish."

Bhasmasur was delighted and said to the god, "Oh Lord, grant me my wish. Let it be that whomever I touch turns to ash."

Now Mahadeva was easily flattered and quick to act. Without thinking, he fulfilled the demon's wish. *"Tathastu,"* he said. "Let it be."

After a few moments, Bhasmasur asked, "Is my wish working?"

"Dear demon," said Mahadeva, "how can you ask such a question? Of course you have the power you requested."

"Oh, Lord," cried Bhasmasur, "how will I know unless I test it? Since there is no one here but you, may I place my hand on your head?"

"Fool!" cried Mahadeva. "Then I will be turned to ash!"

"But, oh Lord," said Bhasmasur, "how will I know if my wish works?"

With that, the demon stepped forward, his hand outstretched toward Mahadeva's head. Mahadeva, frightened, stepped back, and the demon moved forward. Mahadeva, realizing he had made a terrible mistake, tried to escape. He ran to his family in the mountains, but still the demon followed.

When Mahadeva arrived at Mt. Halesi, he dug a hole in the mountain to hide himself and his family, his wife, Parvati, and his son, Ganesh. While he was digging the hole, his mount, the ox Basaha, stood fighting at the entrance of the cave to keep the demon away. But the ox was defeated, and the demon pushed his way downward.

Mahadeva heard the demon coming and began to dig another hole, this time tunneling upward toward the earth's surface. The demon was close behind, so Mahadeva dug another hole, this one going downward. In the bottom of the new hole he hid himself and his family.

Vishnu, the god of preservation, saw what was happening and came to earth in the form of a beautiful maiden. The maiden approached the demon, who was looking tired and sad. "Oh, great demon," she said, "why are you looking so sad?"

"My lady," said Bhasmasur, "Lord Mahadeva has cheated me. He granted me my wish but escaped before I could find out whether it worked."

The maiden laughed out loud.

"Why are you laughing?" asked Bhasmasur.

"Because it is funny, of course," said the maiden. "Why do you have to find someone to test your wish? Why not try it on yourself?"

"How could I do that?" asked Bhasmasur.

"You could put your hand on your own head."

"Ah, what a fool I am," said Bhasmasur. "Why did I not think of that?" Laughing at his own foolishness, Bhasmasur said, "Oh lady, please be my witness and see if my wish works." Bhasmasur then put his hand on his own head and immediately was turned to ash.

Now today, if you go to Mt. Halesi in eastern Nepal, you will see the caves dug by Lord Mahadeva. One is called Basahathan, the place of Basaha who fought the demon. At its entrance is a boulder that looks like an ox. The second cave is called Mahadevathan, the place of Lord Mahadeva. On the floor of this cave are many stalagmites, which people say are the gods who came to visit Lord Mahadeva while he was in hiding. One stalagmite is said to be the lord himself, two others, his wife and son. On the roof of the cave, stalactites drip lime water onto the stalagmites, which people say are offerings of milk from heaven for the visiting gods and goddesses.

About two miles away is a pile of black rocks, said to be the burnt relics of the demon Bhasmasur. So goes the story of the cave of Mt. Halesi.

PLAY WITH THIS STORY

Play ash monster. One person is the ash monster. The ash monster chases after the other children, and anyone touched must freeze and melt to the ground as a pile of ashes. Give the ash monster just one minute to chase. Then stop the game, choose another ash monster, and begin again.

ABOUT THIS STORY

Motif D565 *Transformation by touching*.

This story has similarities with the tale of King Midas, who turned everything that he touched to gold. The motif of turning himself to ash, however, is unique to this tale. This story also includes motif G520 *Ogre deceived into self-injury*.

Mt. Halesi is in the foothills of the Himalayas of eastern Nepal. Lord Mahadeva is another name for Lord Shiva.

THE RIVER KAMALA

The River Kamala is sacred, as are all Nepalese rivers, and considered a source of life. The people of Nepal worship their rivers and do not directly befoul them.

Long ago there lived a *Brahmin* who owned a slave girl named Kamala. Now this Brahmin wanted to make a pilgrimage to India to the holy River Ganges, the holiest of all rivers. His slave girl asked if she too could send an offering. Since she was a slave and owned no property, she asked her mistress for help. The Brahmin's wife agreed and gave Kamala a handful of radish leaves from the garden.

Kamala handed the radish leaves to the Brahmin, saying, "Oh, master, I wish to make an offering of these green leaves to the holy River Ganges. Please carry them with you and offer them to the river."

The Brahmin said to Kamala, "Foolish girl, you would be better off with food or flowers."

"Oh, master," Kamala sighed, "I would like to make an offering of food or flowers, but I cannot afford it."

Though Kamala's offering was poor, the Brahmin took it anyway, promising he would give it to the river. Then he left on his pilgrimage.

Fifteen days later, the Brahmin reached the River Ganges. How great was his joy when he bathed his body in its holy waters and worshipped it with his offerings. The following day he started for home, but to his surprise he discovered that at the end of the day he was in the same place from which he had started. The next day he set off again, but by the end of the day he was back where he had begun. So it happened on the third day. Now the Brahmin was exhausted and did not understand these strange occurrences.

On the fourth day he was about to set off, when he felt in his pocket the dried radish leaves the slave girl had given him. "Oh, dear," said the Brahmin, "I have forgotten to give Kamala's offering." With that, he walked toward the river and threw in the dried radish leaves. To his surprise, a human form emerged from the water, holding the leaves in her hand.

"Who are you, oh goddess?" asked the Brahmin in surprise.

The goddess looked at the dried radish leaves and, with tears in her eyes, said, "I am the River Ganges, sister of your slave girl Kamala. She is the youngest of my sisters and my most beloved. In a former life, she took a loan from you and failed to repay it, so in this life she is destined to be your slave girl. Now she has worked long enough to repay you. Please let her go."

The Brahmin, feeling very sorry he had taken a goddess as his slave, hurried home to release her. As he entered his village, he saw Kamala returning from the water tap. "Holy goddess Kamala!" the Brahmin called out. Kamala turned to see who had called her "goddess." When she saw it was her master, she vanished into air.

The Brahmin hurried to the spot where Kamala had been but saw only a water pot tilted on its side, the water flowing out. Day after day, the water flowed at this spot and was called the holy *River Kamala,* which flowed into the Ganges, the most sacred of all rivers.

To this day one may see a spring flowing out of a pitcher-like rock. The people of the area worship this spring, saying that Kamala is repaying her debt by providing water for them to drink and to irrigate the valley.

PLAY WITH THIS STORY

Trace the river's course. Print out a map of the Ganges River Basin. The Kamala runs into the Kosi River, and this runs into the Ganges. Trace the course of the river with a yellow marker until it reaches the sea.

Show respect to a stream. The Ganges is considered a sacred river in India. Our streams and rivers deserve respect too. Visit a river and float flowers or leaves on the water. Watch it flow and talk about where the water came from and where it is going.

ABOUT THIS STORY

A941.0.1 *Origin of a particular spring.*

The River Kamala is in eastern Nepal between the Mahabharat Range and the Siwalik Mountains. A *Brahmin* is a member of the highest order in the Hindu caste system.

ABOUT THE AUTHORS

KAVITA RAM SHRESTHA was born in the village of Okhaldhunga at the foot of Mt. Everest in eastern Nepal. A sociologist, author, and filmmaker, he is author of 27 books in Nepali, 5 in English, and over 250 journal articles. He has been associated with the Kist Medical College in Nepal and has been a visiting professor at the Department of Public Health, University of Aberdeen, Aberdeen, Scotland.

SARAH LAMSTEIN, a former school librarian, is a puppeteer and an author of children's books, including *Letter on the Wind: A Chanukah Tale*, illustrated by Neil Waldman (Honesdale, PA: Boyds Mills Press, 2008). She became interested in Nepal during a family trip there.

Sarah's Web site is http://sarahlamstein.com.

NETHERLANDS

From *The Flying Dutchman and Other Folktales from the Netherlands* by Theo Meder (Libraries Unlimited, 2008).

HOW THE PEOPLE LEARNED TO EAT POTATOES

These events took place in a time when people were unfamiliar with potatoes. In that time, there lived a minister who was kind of progressive. He tried to stimulate the people to eat potatoes and to cultivate them. He even commenced to grow potatoes on his own acre. However, the people refused to eat things they did not know, and they refused to grow them even more. Nobody fancied potatoes.

Then the minister went to his land and had a sign put there. The sign said that no one was allowed to even touch the potatoes because they were solely for royal consumption. It was royal food. Potatoes were only to be served at the king's table. The sign also mentioned how they had to be prepared.

The minister put a policeman near the field as a guard; he had to see to it that no thieves would steal potatoes. However, the policeman just walked up and down a bit. One moment he was here, the other he was there, and he did not keep a really close watch. People like to do things that are prohibited.

It so happened that every now and again, someone went to the field of potatoes and pulled some potatoes out of the ground, and slowly but surely the number of people doing this increased. First one person ate some potatoes, then another.

That was exactly the intention of the minister. This is how he taught the people to eat potatoes, and everybody liked them so much that they started to grow potatoes themselves the next year.

PLAY WITH THIS STORY

Have a potato-taste test. Purchase a variety of potato types from the grocery. Boil them and cut them in small pieces. Provide toothpicks to stab the potato bits and have a tasting test. Make a chart and let the children decide what categories to put on your chart. Is the texture mushy or hard? What is the color and flavor? Evaluate each potato. Use hatch marks so each child's response can be shown.

You can also vote on the favorite potato. (Note: Please be sure to check on food allergies before offering food to children.)

ABOUT THIS STORY

This story was told on April 27, 1967, to collector A. A. Jaarsma by Mrs. Gesske Kobus-Van der Zee from Nijega, Friesland. It is a version of a tale known as *"Warum die Kartoffeln 'Pfarrerknolln' heissen"* ("Why Potatoes Are Called Minister-turnips").

ABOUT THE AUTHOR

DR. THEO MEDER is the manager of the Dutch Folktale Database, Nederlandse Volksverhalenbank (www.verhalenbank.nl) and the DOC Volksverhaal, a center for folktale research documentation in the Netherlands (www.docvolksverhaal.nl). He is a folk narrative researcher at the Department of Ethnology at the Meertens Institute in Amsterdam and has published many collections of folklore research.

PHILIPPINES

From *Tales from the 7,000 Isles: Filipino Folk Stories* by Dianne de Las Casas and Zarah C. Gagatiga (Libraries Unlimited, 2011).

HOW CRAB GOT ITS EYES
Laguna, Southern Tagalog Region

Tong-tong-tong-tong
Pakitong kitong
Alimango sa dagat (Crab from the sea)
Mabilis at mailap (Swift and fast)
Mahirap mahuli (Hard to catch)
Sapagkat nangangagat! (Careful! The pincers snap!)

The world was young and new. Bathala, the creator, knew that there was still so much work to do. He rolled up his sleeves and started for the seashore.

There, he commanded the wind to stroke the waves so the seawater could carve the land. He instructed the rain to shape the mountains. He called upon the sun to help the plants and trees grow. Very soon, new animals would live and inhabit the forest. Pleased to see the promise of life about him, he began journeying home.

Suddenly, a small animal nudged him on the foot. He looked down at a gray-shelled animal, scurrying to and fro, with no clear direction as to where it wanted to go. Gently, Bathala picked up the creature. The animal's legs wiggled and waggled in the air.

"Ah! Little crab, you seem to be growing very fast!" Bathala exclaimed proudly. He turned Crab around and keenly examined the animal.

"But it seems I have forgotten to give you eyes," Bathala sighed.

"I would really appreciate a pair, Bathala!" Crab replied restlessly.

Bathala opened his left hand and placed Crab carefully in the middle of his palm. Crab was as cold as the water. Bits of sand covered his shell. He scuttled impatiently and would not stay still. Falling from Bathala's cupped hand, Crab landed on the sandy shore on his back. His little legs flailed in the air.

Bathala picked up Crab and securely held the perky animal in his cupped hands. But Crab was impatient. He moved around and around in Bathala's hand. Because Crab was moving about so much, Bathala had difficulty deciding where to put his eyes. Bathala took a deep breath, and with one whoosh, a pair of eyes jutted out of Crab's head.

"I can see now!" Crab cried and jumped down from Bathala's warm hands. He walked sideways with an awkward but swift gait.

"Wait!" Bathala ran after Crab. "Your eyes do not have sockets yet!"

"Just give me pincers, Bathala, so I can use them to bury myself in a hole and catch some food."

"If that is your wish," Bathala replied as he gathered a small mound of sand in his hands.

"Be still," Bathala commanded, but again, Crab would not heed. With a new pair of eyes, he became more excited, moving and scurrying about. Bathala placed his sand-filled hands near his lips as if kissing the grains, then quickly sprinkled the sand on the restless crab. Because Crab would not keep still, the sand landed unevenly. When the pincers appeared, one formed bigger than the other.

Crab tumbled at first but found his balance. Bathala smiled to himself as Crab turned around to thank him. It was a strange animal to look at, but Bathala knew that Crab would thrive despite his imperfections.

PLAY WITH THIS STORY

Make a sandy-backed crab. Shape small crabs from clay. Sprinkle their backs with sand.

ABOUT THIS STORY

Zarah Gagatiga heard this story from her grandmother, Leonida Belmonte. She told the story to demonstrate the importance of listening to one's elders. Versions appear in *Animal Folk Tales from around the World*, vol. 3, by Santhini Govondan (New Delhi: Unicorn Books, no date), and in *Cordillera Tales* by Maria Louisa Agiular-Carino (Quezon City: New Day, 1990).

This study includes several motifs: A2231.1.3 *Discourteous answer: why crab has eyes behind*. Stith Thompson cites versions of this from Estonia and Lithuania. A2376.4 *How crab got its claws*. Stith Thompson shows variants of this tale from India. And A2332.4.2 *Why crab lifts eye out of body or has eye behind*.

JUAN TAMAD AND THE RICE POT
Batangas, Southern Tagalog Region

Juan Tamad was upset. He had been lying the whole morning on the grass under the mango tree with his mouth wide open, waiting for the mango fruit to fall in. However, a *maya* bird came and pecked on the mango fruit he coveted. It was an Indian mango, red, round, and ripe. Juan was too lazy to climb or pick the fruit himself.

So he stood up and took the path that led home. His stomach rumbled. It was nearly noon. Lunchtime! His last meal was breakfast, hours ago. He was cranky and hungry. As he traveled, he smelled something tasty. The scent penetrated his nose and teased his stomach.

"Hmmm. . . ." He sniffed. "*Adobo!* Stewed chicken!"

"Hmmm. . . ." He sniffed again. "Steamed rice!"

He followed the smell. It led him to the doorstep of Aling Nena, his neighbor. He knocked on the door and called for her. There was no answer. "Where could Aling Nena be?" he asked. "She's a good friend of my mother's. She's like an aunt to me. I am sure she won't mind if I come in."

He let himself in the house and walked straight into the kitchen. On his way there, he noticed that a door in one room was left ajar. He took a peek. He saw a rattan hammock. Hunger won over curiosity, so he quickly tiptoed away and into the kitchen. There, he saw a pot filled with steamed rice. Beside it was a *kawali*, a pan, of *adobo*.

"Oh, this means lunch!" Juan shouted with glee. He took a spoon and a plate from a nearby *paminggalan*, a pantry. Just as he was about to get a spoonful of *adobo* and rice, he heard a baby's cry.

He dropped his kitchen utensils and ran to the room where the door was left ajar. There, in the hammock, lay a crying baby. Juan picked up the baby and lulled her to sleep. As he cradled her, he sang,

> *Aya, ayayayaya Neneng!*
> *Meme na!*
> *Aya, ayayayaya Neneng!*
> *Meme na!*

In no time, the baby was asleep. Juan laid her back in the hammock. He ran back to the kitchen and again began to serve himself *adobo* and rice. Just as he was about to get a spoonful of *adobo* and rice from the rice pot, he heard the baby's cry again.

He dropped his kitchen utensils and ran toward the room where the door was left ajar. There, in the hammock, lay the baby still crying. Juan picked up the baby again and lulled her to sleep. As he cradled her, he sang,

> *Aya, ayayayaya Neneng!*
> *Meme na!*
> *Aya, ayayayaya Neneng!*
> *Meme na!*

Then the baby fell asleep once more. Juan laid her back in the hammock. He ran back to the kitchen and began to serve himself *adobo* and rice. Just as he was about to get a spoonful of *adobo* and rice, he heard the baby's cry again.

He dropped his kitchen utensils and ran again to the room where the door was left ajar. Once more, Juan picked up the baby and lulled her to sleep. As he cradled her, he sang,

> *Aya, ayayayaya Neneng!*
> *Meme na!*
> *Aya, ayayayaya Neneng!*
> *Meme na!*

Finally, the baby closed her eyes and fell asleep. He was about to lay the baby back in her hammock when the door opened. In the doorway stood Aling Nena, with her hands on her hips and a stern look on her face.

"*Naku!* Goodness! I shouldn't have left my *apo*, my grandchild!" she fussed.

Juan was nervous. Aling Nena did not look pleased.

"But it's a good thing you're my neighbor, Juan. Thank you so much for looking after Neneng while I was away!" Aling Nena beamed at him.

"Lay her back down in the hammock, Juan, and follow me to the kitchen. I'll give you a bowl of *adobo* and a plate of steamed rice. Bring it home and share it with your mother. I'm sure you will both enjoy my cooking!"

Juan went home happy, with a bowl of *adobo* in one hand and a plate of steamed rice in the other.

PLAY WITH THIS STORY

Act it out. Retell the story letting all of the children except one be the crying babies. The child playing Juan Tamad has to rush around feeding them all every time they cry. You can also act this out as tandem telling, with teams: one child is Juan Tamad, the other is the crying baby. You lead the telling. Tell how Juan goes back to the kitchen to eat and then the baby cries again!

ABOUT THIS STORY

Zarah Gagatga heard this story from her cousin, Analiza Belmonte, from Batangas. The tale also appears in *Legends of Two Peoples* by Benjamin B. Domingo and Eileen Anderson (Manila: FSI, 1983).

Juan Bobo tales (Juan Tamad here) are widespread in Spanish-influenced cultures. Spain ruled the Philippines most of the time from 1565 to 1898 and that culture has had an influence on some of the folklore of the Philippines. Juan Bobo (Juan Tamad) is always a fool, and many stories are told of his bumbling.

ABOUT THE AUTHORS

ZARAH C. GAGATIGA is a school librarian and storyteller. She is active in the Philippine Board on Books for Young People (PBBY). Many of the stories in the book *Tales from the 7,000 Isles: Filipino Folk Stories* are tales Zara heard from her family.

DIANNE DE LAS CASAS lived in the Philippines as a child and enjoyed touring all over the Philippines to collect stories with her coauthor, Zarah Gagatiga. She travels to the Philippines as often as she can and enjoys preserving her cultural heritage through storytelling and writing.

Dianne is an award-winning author, storyteller, and founder of Picture Book Month. Her performances, dubbed "revved-up story-telling," are full of energetic audience participation. The author of 24 books, Dianne is the International Reading Association LEADER 2014 Poet Laureate and the 2014 recipient of the Ann Martin Book Mark Award.

Dianne, born in the Philippines, is a proud Filipina-American. Her Web site is www.story-connection.net.

POLAND

From *Polish Folktales and Folklore*. Retold by Michal Malinowski and Anne Pellowski (Libraries Unlimited, 2009).

COBBLER KOPYTKO AND HIS DUCK KWAK

This is only the first part of a much longer tale. Kopytko means "little last," referring to the shoemaker's last (a form shaped like a human foot on which the shoemaker builds his shoes). The panorama referred to in the first paragraph was an early form of picture show, telling stories by means of a large, rolled series of pictures.

Listen to what happened a hundred and fifty years ago. I saw it with my own eyes. In a town so big it had its own panorama, there lived a cobbler's apprentice whose name was Kopytko. He was so funny it was impossible to look at him without laughing. He would play tricks instead of mending shoes. Each time he played a trick, his master would pull one of his ears. This happened so often that his ears got to be as big as those of an elephant. But Kopytko was glad of that because he could keep a lot of things in his big ears.

In his right ear he had a knife, buttons, chestnuts, and a spool of thread. In his left ear he kept a piece of pitch, a slingshot, and twenty small stones. You know he must have been a naughty youngster if he kept a slingshot and stones.

One evening Kopytko shot a stone so high it hit the moon in its face and knocked out the two front teeth. The poor moon had to hide its face behind the clouds for a night or two. When it reappeared again, it seemed to have a bandage on its face and was no longer smiling.

One time, Kopytko made shoes for a man who was always in a hurry. And do you know what he did? He put the heels where the toes should be and the toes where the heels should be. The man put on his shoes and started to go home to his dinner, but every time he tried to take a step forward, he went backward instead. He could not move from the spot for a long time and almost died of hunger. Kopytko laughed at him until his ears shook.

Sometimes, as punishment, Kopytko did not get any dinner from his master. But that seemed a small punishment for the mean thing he did once to a kind old gentleman. This man came to be measured for new shoes. He had very big feet, so the master called all of his apprentices to help him with the measuring tape. When no one was looking, Kopytko put a crab into the man's pocket. The crab ate a handkerchief, a pair of gloves, and a newspaper. When the man put his hand into that pocket, the crab bit one of his fingers. The man shouted so loud, and the crab squeaked so shrilly, that the master ran away and did not come back.

Kopytko was now left on his own, so he decided to go away. He took with him some of the shoemaker's supplies. He wandered on until he met an enormous duck—a drake. The duck was staggering toward him.

"Why are you waddling like that?" asked Kopytko.

"I am a bit tipsy," said the duck.

"What's your name?' asked Kopytko,

"Kwak!" answered the duck.

"Well, come along with me and we can be merry together," said Kopytko.

"Where are you going?" asked Kwak.

"I'm trying to find a shoemaker, so I can finish my apprenticeship," answered Kopytko.

"All right, I'll go with you," said Kwak. "I have never seen ears like yours before."

Then went along together, playing tricks wherever they stopped. Kwak was as mischievous as Kopytko, perhaps even more so. They walked on and on, until they came to an old man lying down under a tree and fast asleep. He looked like a kindly person because he smiled sweetly in his sleep. Kopytko and Kwak began to plan how they could trick him.

Kopytko quietly approached the man, took off his shoes, tied them to a long piece of his shoemaker's thread, and strung the shoes up over a high branch of the tree. They waited until the man woke up. He looked around, and when he could not find his shoes, he was sure they were stolen. He grew sad, and a few tears fell down his cheeks. Suddenly he looked up and saw his shoes hanging in the air above him. He stretched out his hand to pull them down, but the shoes slid up high into the air. Then they came down again, and once more the man tried to grasp them. But again the shoes went back up high. The old man sat down and began to cry bitterly. The tears poured down his face.

Kopytko, who was hiding behind the tree, whispered to Kwak, "What is happening to his eyes?"

"I don't know," answered Kwak, "but they seem to be quite wet."

"That's the first time I have seen that," said Kopytko. He was so overcome with curiosity that he came out from behind the tree and approached the old man.

"Oh misery and misfortune," cried the old man.

"What has happened?" asked Kopytko.

"My shoes have run away, and they won't come back. I have no money to buy another pair."

"I will bring your shoes back to you," said Kopytko, "if you tell me what that is coming from your eyes."

"Those are tears," answered the old man. "Did you never weep?"

"I don't know how," said Kopytko.

"Do you know how to laugh?"

"Oh, that I can do very well. I do it all the time." He ran behind the tree and brought the old man his shoes. Following him came Kwak.

"Why did you take them from me? Do you need a pair of shoes?'

"No."

"Then why did you do it?"

"To do mischief and give myself a good laugh."

"But that is what caused me to shed tears."

"Do those tears hurt you when you weep?"

"Yes, they hurt very badly. That is why one should never cause others to cry. Now, come near me."

"Are you going to hit me because I played a trick on you?"

"No, I wish to hug you and ask you never to play such tricks that make others cry. Come near me."

Kopytko approached him carefully. The old man patted him on the head and kissed him on both cheeks.

"What is this?" asked Kopytko in wonder as he felt something on his cheeks.

"Those are tears, and that means you have learned to cry."

"But you told me that tears cause pain, and these don't hurt me. In fact, they feel quite nice."

"That's because they are tears of joy. When you are very, very happy, you often cry tears of joy. Please don't play anymore tricks that cause tears of pain."

"But I have always been merry. It is the way I am."

"That is fine," said the old man. "It is good to be merry and bring laughter to the world. Just don't bring it at someone else's expense. From now on, do your tricks and merry making out in the open, *for* others but not *to* others. You will see how much fun you can have." The old man went off with a smile.

"I liked that old man," said Kwak.

Kopytko and Kwak walked on until they came to the edge of a forest. There stood two children, crying because they had lost their way.

"Go near them and dance on one foot," Kopytko ordered Kwak. "I will stand on my head and kick my feet." They danced and kicked until the children stopped crying and started laughing. Then they helped the children find their way home. The parents hugged and kissed Kopytko and Kwak and gave them something to eat. Both of them felt really good.

They continued on their way and met a beggar, sitting at a crossroads and moaning.

"What's the matter?" asked Kopytko.

"I'm hungry and unhappy."

Kopytko reached into his ears, but he could find no food. Then he ordered Kwak to dance the Krakowiak, a lively dance. Kwak put out one of his feet and turned in a circle on the other. He turned and capered so much the beggar started to laugh. He laughed so hard he forgot he was hungry.

"How strange, he seems to have satisfied his hunger with laughter. Can laughter be eaten, I wonder?" asked Kwak.

"It seems to be very healthy," answered Kopytko.

Thus they traveled for weeks and months. Whenever they heard of a person suffering sadness or sorrow, they went as quickly as possible to cheer up that person. In a short time, they became famous in the whole country and were blessed everywhere.

PLAY WITH THIS STORY

Make someone laugh. Let two children be Kopytko and Kwak. The other children can pretend to be very sad. Kopytko and Kwak dance and cavort to make them laugh.

Make sad and happy faces. Pass out two circles to each child. Let children draw happy and sad faces. Decorate the faces by pasting on curled paper for hair.

ABOUT THIS STORY

Many tales are told in which people are compelled to laugh or dance by playing a magic instrument. These are motifs D1415 *Magic object compels person to dance* and D1419.1 *Magic object compels person to laugh*. However, in this tale, people laugh just at seeing Kopytko and Kwak perform.

WHERE IS THE WOLF?

This rhyme is either simply recited, with the adult pretending to "eat" the child's body by kissing it in many places, or someone performs the actions stated here. This rhyme is also used by older children when playing a circle game.

> Where is the wolf? Running in the hills.
> What is he doing? Chasing the geese.
> Has he found many? More than twenty.
> How are his eyes?
> Like coals in the night skies. [Form circles around eyes.]
> How are his ears?
> Like spears that one fears. [Point a finger above each ear.]
> How is his nose?
> Like the end of a hose. [Make circle around nose.]
> How are his front paws?
> Like wood-cutting saws. [Move arms in saw-cutting motion.]
> How are his hind legs?
> Like two huge wooden pegs. [Move legs stiffly.]
> How is his snout?
> Big! The better to eat you, no doubt! [Make smacking noises all over child's body.]

PLAY WITH THIS STORY

Recite a tickling rhyme. If telling the story to just one or two children, the adult can pretend to "eat" the child's body by kissing it in many places as the story unfolds.

Recite an action rhyme. Lead the children in carrying out the actions called for.

Play a circle game. This rhyme is also used by older children when playing a circle game. On the last line they attack each other with snapping jaws (extended arms).

ABOUT THIS STORY

This story is related to motif Z18.1 *What makes your ears so big? To hear the better, my child, etc.* Type 333. This motif appears in the Red Riding Hood tale, but it also appears alone elsewhere, as in this chant.

ABOUT THE AUTHORS

MICHAL MALINOWSKI founded and directs the Storytelling Museum in Konstancin-Jeziorna, near Warsaw. He organizes a storytelling festival in Poland and arranges storytelling events throughout the country. He also collects folktales from tellers throughout the country. Born in Warsaw, Michal graduated from the Academy of Fine Arts in Lausanne and studied folklore and mythology at Harvard. You can hear an interview with Michal at http://www.artofstorytellingshow.com/2009/12/16/michal-malinowski-storytelling-museum-poland.

ANNE PELLOWSKI grew up in a large Polish American community in Pine Creek, Wisconsin. She is author of a series of children's books about five generations of her Polish family, the Latsch Valley Farm series: *Winding Valley Farm: Annie's Story* (Bethlehem Books, 2009); *Stairstep Farm: Anna Rosa's Story* (Bethlehem Books, 2011); *First Farm in the Valley: Anna's Story* (Bethlehem Books, 2012); and *Willow Wind Farm: Betsy's Story* (Bethlehem Books, 2012). Anne lives now in Winona, Minnesota, and travels widely throughout the world offering storytelling workshops.

RUSSIA

From *The Snow Maiden and Other Russian Tales* Translated and Retold by Bonnie C. Marshall (Libraries Unlimited, 2004).

THE MANSION-HOUSE

A peasant was riding along with a cartload of crockery when one of the jugs fell from the top of the cart and rolled to the side of the road. The peasant, not noticing that he had lost one of his wares, traveled on.

Sorrowful the Fly was flying by, and she caught sight of the jug. "Whose mansion-house is this?" she asked. "Who lives here?"

No one answered. There was no one at home, so Sorrowful the Fly flew into the jug and set up housekeeping.

The next day Whiner the Mosquito flew up to the jug and asked, "Whose mansion-house is this? Who lives here?"

"I do, Sorrowful the Fly. And who are you?"

"I am Whiner the Mosquito."

"Why not come in and live with me?" asked Sorrowful the Fly.

Whiner the Mosquito accepted the invitation gladly, and the two insects began living together in peace and harmony.

Nibbles the Mouse was taking a stroll when she spied the jug. "Whose mansion-house is this?" she asked. "Who lives here?"

A tiny voice answered, "We do, Sorrowful the Fly and Whiner the Mosquito. And who are you?"

"I am Nibbles the Mouse."

"Come live with us, Nibbles."

Nibbles the Mouse went inside, and all three creatures began living together.

The next day Croaker the Frog came hopping up to the mansion-house. She asked, "Whose mansion-house is this? Who lives here?"

"I do, Sorrowful the Fly."

"I do, Whiner the Mosquito."

"And I do, Nibbles the Mouse. And who are you?"

"I am Croaker the Frog."

"Do come live with us, Croaker," said the inhabitants of the jug.

The frog hopped into the jug happily, and the four of them began living together.

Soon afterwards Skipper the Rabbit hopped past the jug. He caught sight of it and asked, "Whose mansion-house is this? Who lives here?"

"I do, Sorrowful the Fly."

"I do, Whiner the Mosquito."

"I do, Nibbles the Mouse."

"I do, Croaker the Frog. And who are you?"

"I am Skipper the Rabbit."

"Come join us, friend!" said the inhabitants of the jug.

The rabbit skipped into the jug, and all five friends began living together.

Soon, along came Sister Fox. She knocked on the side of the jug and asked, "Whose mansion-house is this? Who lives here?"

"I do, Sorrowful the Fly."

"I do, Whiner the Mosquito."

"I do, Nibbles the Mouse."

"I do, Croaker the Frog."

"I do, Skipper the Rabbit. And who are you?"

"I am silver-tongued Sister Fox."

"Come live with us, Sister Fox," said the inhabitants of the jug.

The fox climbed into the jug, and all six friends began living happily together.

That night Gray-legs the Wolf came by. He looked into the opening of the jug and asked, "Whose mansion-house is this? Who lives here?"

"I do, Sorrowful the Fly."

"I do, Whiner the Mosquito."

"I do, Nibbles the Mouse."

"I do, Croaker the Frog."

"I do, Skipper the Rabbit."

"I do, Sister Fox. And who are you?"

"I am Gray-legs the Wolf."

"Well, come live with us, Gray-legs!"

The wolf climbed into the jug. Although it was becoming a little crowded to say the least, all seven friends began living together in happiness and harmony. They sang songs and made merry all day long.

One day Fumble Paws the Bear heard singing coming from the jug. He stopped short and roared with all his might, "Whose mansion-house is this? Who lives here?"

"I do, Sorrowful the Fly."

"I do, Whiner the Mosquito."

"I do, Nibbles the Mouse."

"I do, Croaker the Frog."

"I do, Skipper the Rabbit."

"I do, Sister Fox."

"I do, Gray-legs the Wolf. And who are you?"

"I am Fumble Paws the Bear."

"Come live with us, Fumble Paws."

"Why, thank you," said the bear. He tried to crawl into the jug. He pushed, and he pushed. He snorted and groaned, but he could not squeeze into the jug.

"I had better sit on top of the jug," he decided.

Fumble Paws the Bear climbed onto the top of the jug. No sooner did he sit down than smash—he squashed the jug to pieces!

As the jug was falling apart, there was barely enough time for Sorrowful the Fly, Whiner the Mosquito, Nibbles the Mouse, Croaker the Frog, Skipper the Rabbit, Sister Fox, and Gray-legs the Wolf to escape unharmed. All of the creatures living in the jug ran off to the forest, where they searched for a new home.

PLAY WITH THIS STORY

Make a cardboard jug house. Fold a piece of cardboard in half, trace a jug form on it (with the top of the jug at the paper's opening, give it a broad mouth), cut this out and staple the sides. Give

---

each child one of these plus cut outs of the fly, mosquito, mouse, frog, rabbit, fox and wolf. Retell the story putting each animal into the "jug". Use your fist as the bear to squash the jug and all inside.

Compare with Other Tales

Compare with one of these picture book retellings of "The Mitten." *The Mitten* by Jan Brett (Hodder Wayland, 1999) (Ukrainian); *The Mitten* by Alvin Tresselt and Yaroslava (HarperCollins, 1989); *The Mitten* by Jim Aylesworth, illus. Barbara McClintock (Scholastic, 2009).

For yet another variant of this story see: "Who Lives in the Skull?" in *When the Lights Go Out* by Margaret Read MacDonald (H.W. Wilson, 1988), pp.143–147. (Russian).

ABOUT THIS STORY

J2199.5.2* *Mouse makes home in mitten*. Versions from Russia and Ukraine. A similar story from Scotland shows people crowding into a house until it bursts. *Always Room for One More* by Sorche Nic Leodhas, illus. Nonny Hogrogian (New York: Rinehart & Winston, 1965).

THE WINGED, HAIRY, AND BUTTERY FRIENDS

At the edge of the forest in a warm little cottage, there once lived three friends—a winged sparrow, a hairy mouse, and a buttery pancake called a *blin*. The three had met and become friends after the sparrow flew in from the field, the mouse escaped the cat, and the *blin* ran away from the frying pan.

The sparrow, the mouse, and the *blin* lived together in friendship, never hurting one another's feelings. Each one did his work and helped the others. The sparrow brought his friends food. He brought grain from the fields, mushrooms from the forest, and beans from the garden. The mouse chopped wood, and the *blin* cooked cabbage soup and a porridge called kasha.

So, the three friends lived in harmony. Their routine was like this. After the sparrow returned home from hunting for food, he would wash up with well water and sit on the bench to rest. The mouse would drag in the wood, set the table, and count the painted spoons. Ruddy and fluffy, the *blin* would stand beside the stove salting the cabbage soup and testing the kasha.

When the friends sat down to eat, they could not praise the *blin* enough. The sparrow would say, "Oh, what wonderful cabbage soup. It's fit for nobility, so tasty and rich it is."

The *blin* would reply. "I am a buttery pancake. I plunged into the pot and climbed out again. That is why the cabbage soup is rich."

The sparrow would eat the kasha, praising it, too. "Oh, what splendid kasha this is. It is piping hot."

The mouse would say, "I brought in the wood. I gnawed it into tiny pieces, threw it into the stove, and scattered it around with my tail. That caused it to burn well in the stove. That's why the kasha is hot."

"I was Johnny-on-the-spot, too," the sparrow would say. "I gathered the mushrooms and brought in the beans. That's why you're not hungry."

Thus they lived, praising themselves and one another, and taking no offense.

One day the sparrow became thoughtful. "I fly around the forest all day long," he thought. "I beat my legs and wear out my wings. And what are my friends doing? The *blin* lolls on the stove all morning luxuriating and sets about making dinner only toward evening.

In the morning the mouse carries in wood and gnaws it. Then, she hops up on the stove and turns over on her side and sleeps until dinnertime. But I hunt for food from morning till night. It's hard work. There is no harder work."

The more the sparrow thought, the angrier he got. He stamped his feet, flapped his wings, and began crying, "Tomorrow we'll exchange jobs."

That is just what they did. The *blin* and the mouse understood that it could not be helped, so they decided to swap places. The next morning the *blin* went hunting for food, the sparrow went to chop wood, and the mouse was to cook dinner.

The *blin* rolled off to the forest. It rolled down the road singing:

> Hip-hop, hip-hop,
> I am buttery sides,
> And I can't stop.
> I'm mixed with sour cream
> And fried in butter.
> Hip-hop, hip-hop,
> I am a butterball,
> And I can't stop.

He ran on and met up with Patrikeevna the Fox.

"Where are you rushing, little *blin*?"

"I'm going hunting."

"What was that song you were singing, little *blin*?"

The pancake hopped in place and began singing:

> Hip-hop, hip-hop,
> I am buttery sides,
> And I can't stop.
> I'm mixed with sour cream
> And fried in butter.
> Hip-hop, hip-hop,
> I am a butterball,
> And I can't stop,

"You sing very well," said Patrikeevna the Fox as she drew closer to the *blin*. "You say you were mixed with sour cream?"

"With sour cream and sugar," the *blin* answered.

"Hip-hop, you say?" asked the fox. Then she leapt and gave a snort. She snapped her teeth down on the pancake's buttery side.

"Let me go so that I can go to the deep woods to fetch mushrooms and beans," cried the *blin*. "Let me go hunting for food."

"No, I won't let you go," said the fox. "I'll eat you up, gobble you down, sour cream, butter, sugar, and all."

The *blin* struggled and struggled, and scarcely managed to break away from the fox. A piece of its side remained in the fox's teeth, but the rest of the *blin* ran home.

Meanwhile, at home the mouse was cooking cabbage soup. Whatever she put into the soup, whatever she added, made no difference. The soup was not rich, nor tasty, nor buttery.

"How did the *blin* cook cabbage soup?" wondered the mouse. "Oh, yes, now I remember. It dove into the pot and swam around. Then the soup became rich."

The mouse flung herself into the pot. She was scalded terribly. She barely hopped out alive. Her fur coat fell off, and her little tail trembled. She sat on the wooden bench and wept streams of tears.

The sparrow went after wood. He fetched the wood and dragged it home. Then, he began pecking at it in an attempt to break it into tiny pieces. He pecked and pecked until his beak turned to the side. He sat on the *zavalinka,* which is a mound of earth piled around a Russian peasant cottage to protect against severe weather, and wept streams of tears.

The *blin* came running home and saw the sparrow sitting on the *zavalinka* with his beak twisted to one side and weeping.

The *blin* ran into the cottage and saw the mouse sitting on the bench without her fur coat and with her tail trembling. When the mouse saw that the *blin's* side was eaten away, she wept all the louder.

"This is what happens when one lays blame on another and doesn't want to do his own work," said the *blin.*

In shame, the sparrow took refuge beneath the wooden bench.

Nothing was to be done. The friends wept and grieved. Then, they began living again in the old manner. The sparrow fetched the food. The mouse chopped the wood. The *blin* prepared the cabbage soup and kasha.

Thus they live to this day, gnawing on honey cakes, drinking mead, and remembering you and me.

PLAY WITH THIS STORY

Bake a *blin*! Barbara Marshall gives the recipe for making *bliny* (pancakes) in her book, *The Snow Maiden*. A single pancake is called a *blin*, the plural is *bliny*.

Russian Pancakes (Blini)
Ingredients:
2–3 eggs
3 cups warm water
½ teaspoon salt
1 tablespoon sugar
½ teaspoon baking soda
3 ¾ cups flour

The Winged, Hairy, and Buttery Friends

½ teaspoon lemon juice
1 cup water
Vegetable oil for frying
Butter, sour cream, jam for topping

Directions:
Beat the eggs into 3 cups of warm water. Add salt, sugar, and baking soda. Beat the flour into the mixture until there are no lumps. Mix lemon juice into a cup of water and pour it into the dough and beat. Fry the pancakes (blini) in a frying pan. Keep the bottom of the pan covered with vegetable oil. Serve with butter, sour cream, and jam to spread on top!

Compare with Another Tale

See also "The Little Round Bun," a Ukrainian folktale on page 165. Several more variant picture books are listed on page 168.

ABOUT THIS STORY

Z33.1 *The fleeing pancake. A woman makes a pancake which flees. Various animals try in vain to stop it. Finally the fox eats it up.* Type 2025.

This is a popular tale throughout Europe. MacDonald's *Storyteller's Sourcebook* cites sources from England, Ireland, The Netherlands, Russia, Scotland, and the United States.

MacDonald and Sturm's *Storyteller's Sourcebook: 1983–1999* adds more British sources and a Norwegian version: *The Pancake Boy: An Old Norwegian Folk Tale* by Lorinda Bryan Cauley (New York: Putnam, 1988).

This story has some interesting additions to the usual Z33.1 story. The animals chat about who contributed to the dish, which is reminiscent of the story of "The Little Red Hen," where the animals *refuse* to contribute. Here it is the opposite. See p. 51 for a Haitian version of this motif.

Mouse's claim that he jumped into the pot to flavor the soup reminds us of the Indonesian story on page 67, "Why Shrimps Are Crooked." This is probably an example of similar motifs springing up in the minds of tellers in far-flung corners of the globe.

ABOUT THE AUTHOR

BONNIE C. MARSHALL is a translator and professor of Russian languages at Johnson C. Smith University, who has made many trips to study folklore in the Soviet Union.

She collaborated on this collection with the Russian folklorist Alla V. Kulagina of Moscow State University. Kulagina was born in the Primorskii Territory of the Russian Far East and travels annually with her students to collect folklore from Russia's remote regions.

SAUDI ARABIA

From *Tales from the Arabian Peninsula* by Nadia Jameel Taibah and Margaret Read MacDonald (Libraries Unlimited, 2015).

JOUHA AND HIS DONKEYS

Once Jouha was driving ten donkeys loaded with goods to the city. He loaded up ten donkeys, put them in a line, and counted them out. One, two, three, four, five, six, seven, eight, nine, ten.

Then Jouha got onto one of the donkeys and set off for town. But after a while, it occurred to him that he had better look behind and count to make sure all the donkeys were still in line. To his horror he could only see NINE donkeys behind him!

He got off and checked each donkey carefully. But now there were indeed ten donkeys.

Relieved, he got back on his donkey and continued on his way.

After he had ridden for a while, he realized he should check again to make sure all the donkeys were still following. But "Oh no!" One was missing again!

He jumped down and ran back to line them up and check to see which was missing. But there were ten there after all. Such a problem!

After repeating this several times, it finally dawned on Jouha that everytime he RODE on a donkey, one of the others would slip off. So he sighed and got down from his donkey.

"I will just have to walk," he decided. "It is better to walk on foot and keep all my donkeys than to mount and lose one of them." So he walked all the way to town.

PLAY WITH THIS STORY

Count to 10 in Arabic. Learn to count to 10 in Arabic. You can find pronunciation from Nadia Taibah at www.margaretreadmacdonald.com. Click on "Books & Media." Type in *How Many Donkeys.*"

The book description includes a link to Nadia's voice counting to 10 in Arabic. See also the picture book version of this story, *How Many Donkeys? An Arabic Counting Tale* by Nadia Taibah and Margaret Read MacDonald (Chicago: Albert Whitman, 2012). This includes the Arabic numerals as well as the pronunciation. Note that you read from right to left in Arabic.

Act it out. Now that you can count to 10 in Arabic, line up 10 students as donkeys and act the story out. Lead the donkeys around the room. Stop every so often to count. Let the audience shout, "Count Again, Jouha!"

ABOUT THIS STORY

This story includes motif J2031.0.3 *Counting wrong by not counting self.* MacDonald's *Storyteller's Sourcebook* gives sources from England, Ireland, Denmark, Ethiopia, Sri Lanka, the Philippines, Syria, Turkey, and Armenia and Jewish variants. It is also Type 1287 *Numskulls unable to Count their own Number.* The Aarne-Thompson Type Index gives versions of this story from Turkey, Finland, Sweden, Lithuania, Norway, Ireland, England, France, Spain, the Netherlands, Germany, Hungary, Slovenia, Serbocroation, Russia, India, and Indonesia. A similar tale is told in England of five fishermen: *Five Silly Fishermen* by Roberta Edwards, illustrated by Sylvie Wickstrom (New York: Random House, 1989).

THE POOR LADY'S PLAN

Long, long time ago, there was an old poor lady who lived in a very poor hut. The only thing she had was an old rug covering the floor of her hut. She had a very wealthy neighbor, the head judge of Mecca town. This poor lady used to go every day to the farmers' market to trade her own products for food. She had an old sack that she used to carry on her back so she could carry the vegetables from the market. One day this poor lady came from the market and she found out that her only rug was not on the floor.

She said to herself, "I am sure I didn't move it. Or maybe I sold it and I forgot." While she was looking around for the rug she noticed that the rug was rolled up at one of the dark corners of her poor hut. Well, she was surprised. She was sure that she had not cleaned her house for a long time. And all of the sudden she noticed big filthy shoes coming out of the rug. "My dear Allah" she thought, "here is a burglar, and I am an old lady, ALL ALONE BY MYSELF. Now if I tried to run away, he would definitely catch me. If I screamed nobody is going to hear me before he comes out and kills me." The old poor lady kept thinking and thinking. She was so terrified.

Finally she arrived at this brilliant idea: "Mmmm . . . I will bring my drums and start singing with a loud voice like I am having a party." So she started singing with the old sack filled with vegetables on her back.

Ajoza fi dahraha bostan ya rabee kelkata alrahman
Ajoza fi dahraha bostan ya rabee kelkata alrahman
Ajoza fi dahraha bostan ya rabee kelkata alrahman
(Which means an old lady with garden on her back and that is Allah's creation.)

At that moment the servant of the judge's family was depluming and cleaning a goose for lunch by the kitchen window. She heard the voice of the old poor lady. "Since I started working at the judge's family, I have not been able to have any fun," the servant thought. "It has been a long time since I attended any parties, singing or dancing. I am just going to join the old lady and have some fun." She left everything, the goose, the cooking, and she went to sing and dance.

Kunt Bantuf Alweza we jet Anhazalli Hazza
Kunt Bantuf Alweza we jet Anhazalli Hazza
Kunt Bantuf Alweza we jet Anhazalli Hazza
(Which means I was depluming the goose and I came to dance.)

The singing became a little louder.

The judge's wife was just finishing her cup of coffee and she needed more, so she called the servant to bring her more coffee. "Hey, servant, servant, servant!" with a loud voice she shouted, but nobody answered.

On her way to the kitchen, looking for the servant, she heard singing voices coming from the old lady's hut. She looked from the window and saw the two ladies. The servant and her neighbor were singing and dancing. The wife felt very sorry about herself.

"Since I got married to this judge, I have not been able to attend any wedding or parties," the wife thought. "I need to go with them to sing and dance. Let us have some fun! Who needs to eat or drink!"

> *Sebt Alqahwa wa Alfinjan We Jeet Arqos Fi Almeedan*
> *Sebt Alqahwa wa Alfinjan We Jeet Arqos Fi Almeedan*
> *Sebt Alqahwa wa Alfinjan We Jeet Arqos Fi Almeedan*
> (Which means I left the coffee and the cup and came to dance in field.)

The singing became much louder.

It was time for the judge to come home for lunch. He knocked at the door, calling for his wife or the servant. But nobody was there. "That is strange," the judge said. "Where is everybody? Hey lady! Hey servant!" Nobody answered; so he went to the kitchen, following the loud singing voice.

He saw from the kitchen window his wife, the servant, and the old lady singing and dancing. "Since I became the judge of Mecca, I have not been able to have some time off to myself," the judge grunted. "I really forgot how people sing or dance. I am just going to go and have some fun, singing and dancing with my wife. Losing respect for a while is not really a big deal." So he went wearing his own *kaffieh,* singing with his hoarse voice.

> *Ana Alqadi Bi emmati Wa Jeet Arqos Maa' meerati*
> *Ana Alqadi Bi emmati Wa Jeet Arqos Maa' meerati*
> *Ana Alqadi Bi emmati Wa Jeet Arqos Maa' meerati*
> (Which means I am the judge with my *kaffieh* come to dance with my wife.)

The burglar heard the voice and the identity of the last singer. He got frightened and rolled himself out of the rug and tried to run as quickly as possible.

But the old lady started screaming, "A burglar, a burglar!"

The judge was faster. He caught the burglar and put him into jail! The old lady's plan worked very well.

PLAY WITH THIS STORY

Make a tambourine (or drum). Punch holes in plastic coffee can lids. Provide tiny bells for the children to tie to lids. Play your tambourines and dance. Or make a coffee can drum. The coffee can is already a drum. Just cover its sides with colorful paper and decorate.

Act it out. Make up your own song to sing for each character that enters. Play your tambourines (or use drums) and dance as each new character comes in.

ABOUT THIS STORY

This story includes several motifs: K606.0.3 *Trickster, pretending not to see attacking enemy, sings song.* Similar tales are told in which the person being approached by the burglar innocently sings a song or makes a statement that alarms the burglar or monster and causes him to flee. J2633 *Tiger frightened of leak in house. Overhears householder say he fears "leak."* And N392.1.1 *Thief falls by accident on tiger's back and is carried away. Each thinks other is terrible "leak" which they overheard householder say he feared.* MacDonald's *Storyteller's Sourcebook* cites variants of this from India and China. Also N611.1 *Criminal accidentally detected. "That is the first."* Robber hears and thinks self detected, flees. There are variants from India, China, the United States, Norway, Arabia, Persia, Rumania, Russia, and Spain. And N612 *Numskull talks to himself and frightens robbers away.* MacDonald cites variants of this from Germany, Burma, and Korea. However, in this Saudi tale, the old woman *plans* to frighten the robber.

ABOUT THE AUTHOR

Nadia Jameel Taibah heard stories from her family as she was growing up in Jeddah, Saudi Arabia. The story of counting donkeys was told by her Aunt Salha. Nadia teaches in the education department at King Abdul-Aziz University in Jeddah, Saudi Arabia. She received her doctorate in special education from the University of Washington. Nadia was a preschool teacher before coming to the United States to work on her PhD and told many stories to the children she taught.

SIBERIA

From *Far North Tales: Stories from the Peoples of the Arctic Circle.* Translated and retold by Bonnie C. Marshall. Edited by Kira Van Deusen (Libraries Unlimited, 2011).

WHO SHALL I BE?
Siberian Yupik

A bear cub by the name of Kainekhak became very stubborn and refused to obey his parents. "I don't want to be a bear anymore," he said. "I want to be someone else."

After uttering these words, he ran away from home. He wandered on and finally came to the treeless plain known as the tundra. The sun was shining, and there were many beautiful flowers covering the earth. A ground squirrel was sitting beside her burrow with her front paws hanging down, leaning for support on her tail, and whistling as if she were singing a song.

"I want to stand rooted to the ground, too, so that I can whistle like the ground squirrel," said the cub.

Kainekhak got up onto a little knoll. He let his front paws hang down and leaned on his tail, just as the ground squirrel had done. Then he began whistling. Instead of a whistle, a tremendous roar came out of his mouth. The ground squirrel got scared and ran away.

The little bear cub was annoyed. He wandered on further and came to a herd of grazing deer. He went up to one of them and asked, "Who are you? I've never seen an animal wearing such a head of antlers before."

"I am a deer."

"I want to be a deer, too."

"All right. It will be more enjoyable to have a friend," said the deer. "Let's run and see who is faster."

While the bear cub was huffing and puffing and hobbling along on his crooked paws, the deer disappeared without a trace.

"It's not so interesting being a deer," Kainekhak mumbled, and he walked on.

He came to a lake. Not far from the lake, he caught sight of a duck. "It would be better if I became a duck," decided Kainekhak. "The duck doesn't walk as fast as the deer, and she knows how to fly."

The bear cub stood on his back paws and waved his front paws as if they were wings. He jumped into the air with all his might—and dropped with a thud onto the ground.

"Let me teach you the right way to fly," the duck proposed. "Go over to the cliff by the shore of the lake, and it will be easier to begin."

The duck went up to the very edge of the cliff, spread her wings, and glided over the water.

Kainekhak followed her. He went to the steepest part of the cliff and leapt into the air. He glided down-down-down—and plopped into the water. He fell head first into the lake and began flailing about with his paws. He swallowed water and snorted it out. The bear cub barely made it back to dry land, where he stood shaking the water off for a long time. The water was ice cold and his teeth were chattering, so the little bear cub found no pleasure in his swim.

He dragged himself away and walked on. Suddenly, he met up with his father and mother and brother. He had never been so happy to see them as he was at that moment.

The little family walked on together in the direction of a berry patch. They were chatting and laughing.

"It's better to be a good bear than to disgrace oneself in front of other animals," Kainekhak decided. From then on, he had no desire to be anyone other than what he was—a bear.

PLAY WITH THIS STORY

Act it out. Add other forest animals for Little Bear to meet. What animals might he meet in a Siberian landscape?

Write your own story based on this folktale pattern. This theme of a small animal imitating every animal it meets is used repeatedly in picture books. Decide on a setting for your story and make up your own version of this tale.

ABOUT THIS STORY

This is a Yupik tale from *The Eskimos of Siberia: Part 3* by Vladimir Bogoraz (Waldemar Bogoras). The Jessup North Pacific Expedition. Memoir of the American Museum of Natural History. Volume 8. (Leiden and New York, 1913.) It was told by Kivagmé and recorded by K. Sergeeva.

The tale includes Motif J2413 *Foolish imitation by an animal. Tries to go beyond his powers.* And Motif J512 *Animal should not try to change his nature.* J512

WHY RABBIT HAS LONG EARS
Mansi

When animals first appeared in the forest, Elk was thought to be the oldest and wisest of them all. One day Elk was talking to his wife when Rabbit came running. Rabbit heard their voices and stopped.

"I'll just listen to what they are saying," he said. He sneaked up closer, hid behind a tree stump, and listened.

"I have some antlers here," said Elk, "which I must give to the animals. But there are many animals and few antlers. To whom shall I give them?"

Rabbit listened and thought, "I would like to have those antlers. I am no less deserving than the other animals."

"To whom shall I give the antlers?" Elk repeated.

Rabbit was on the point of opening his mouth to shout, "Give me the antlers!" when Elk's wife suggested, "Give the antlers to Reindeer. He is your relative, so you should give them to him."

"All right," said Elk. "Here are some antlers for Reindeer. Now who else should get a pair of antlers?"

Elk's wife was just about to answer when Rabbit, unable to bear it any longer, leaned out from behind the tree stump and shouted, "Give them to me, Elk!"

"What sort of idea is that, brother?" asked Elk. "Why do you need such big antlers? What would you do with them?"

"What would I do with them?" Rabbit repeated Elk's question. "Why, I need antlers to scare my enemies so that they will fear me."

"Well, then, all right, take them," said Elk, and he gave Rabbit the antlers.

Rabbit was overjoyed. He put the antlers on and began jumping and dancing around. Suddenly, a big cone fell from the cedar tree right onto his head.

Rabbit jumped up in fright and began running. He made a dash but came to a crashing stop. He had not gotten very far. His antlers had become entangled in some bushes. Unable to get free, he began squealing fearfully and trembling all over.

Elk and his wife laughed. "No, brother," said wise Elk, "antlers are not for the likes of you. The longest antlers in the world won't help a coward. Give them back to me and take these long ears instead, so that everyone will know that you are an eavesdropper who likes to listen to what other people are saying."

That is how snoopy Rabbit lost his antlers. The ears that Elk gave him grew and grew. Every time Rabbit listened to words that were not meant for him, his ears became a little longer.

PLAY WITH THIS STORY

Make antlers. Use brown construction paper to make large antlers. Fasten them to a construction paper headband and wear them to prance around the room. Are they a nuisance to wear? Play a game like London Bridge Is Falling Down and notice how much the antlers get in the way.

ABOUT THIS STORY

The authors tell us that the elk in this story is a European elk and thus more similar to the American moose.

This is Motif A2325.1 *Why rabbit has long ears.*

ABOUT THE AUTHORS

BONNIE C. MARSHALL is a Russian-language scholar. She selected and translated these tales.

KIRA VAN DEUSEN is a Canadian storyteller who has traveled widely in Siberia collecting tales.

Kira's Web site is http://kiravan.com/performance.html.

Photo by Jasmin Dzin

SOUTH AMERICA

From *Pachamama Tales: Folklore from Argentina, Bolivia, Chile, Paraguay, Peru, and Uruguay* by Paula Martín. Edited by Margaret Read MacDonald (Libraries Unlimited, 2014).

THE MONKEY AND THE YACARÉ

A Guaraní folktale from Paraguay and Corrientes Province, Argentina. For a Spanish text of this tale see Pachamama Tales, *pp. 27–29*

The Yacaré is a caiman that can be six to eight feet long. They live in rivers of Argentina, eastern Bolivia, Paraguay, Uruguay, and Brazil—especially the Pantanal region of Brazil. This story has some unusual Paraguayan Guaraní words in it. It is more fun to just play with them, rather than making up a translation. A "guaina" is a young girl.

There once was a monkey who wanted to cross the river to get to a big party that was taking place on the other bank. He was afraid to cross, not only because he didn't know how to swim, but also because a huge *yacaré* lived on the riverbank. From the top of a tree the monkey called to the *yacaré* to see if the alligator would help him cross the river.

"How are you doing *chamigo*! The other day a *guaina* was asking for you."

"Really? And what did she say?"

"She said that you are a very good looking and elegant lad."

The *yacaré* shook its tale from joy.

"Really? Which one? Which young woman? Please tell me!"

"That one! The one that lives there on the other side of the river and that is very beautiful."

"I don't know which one. You tell me."

"What a pity! Just now she is having a party at her house. But since I can't cross the river, I can't introduce her to you."

"I can get you to the other side! Climb up my back carefully and I will take you."

"Is it safe?"

"Of course, you are not going to tell me that you are afraid of the water, are you?"

"Nnn no . . . of course not."

The monkey climbed up carefully onto the back of the alligator. He was trembling from fright while the alligator shook itself with enthusiasm.

"While I cross over, tell me what else she said about me."

"That you are nice looking, a good swimmer. . . ."

"Ha, ha, ha . . . I like that," said the alligator, and from happiness he kept on shaking his tail and wanted to hear more. Monkey, full of fear, kept on inventing.

"What else? What else?"

"That you have nice eyes, soft skin, that you know how to sing and dance. . . ."

"Ha, ha, ha . . . I like that," said the alligator, while he shook his tail even more, and the monkey trembled, more and more frightened.

Since the river was very wide, the alligator kept on asking, "And what else did the *guaina* say about me?"

"That you are brave, that you are a good worker, and that you are so romantic. . . ."

"Ha, ha, ha . . . I like that," repeated the alligator and shook itself so much that the monkey barely knew how to remain on its back, but he wouldn't do or say anything, afraid of falling into the water.

When they finally arrived at the other side of the river, the alligator asked once more, "Before you introduce me to her, tell me, what else did she say about me?"

First the monkey gave a great leap to firm ground. Then he quickly climbed a tree. When he saw that he was high enough to be safe, he yelled, "This is what she said about you:

> *Ese tobá mocái, acä chipá guazú,*
> *jheté curú,*
> *rezá guazú,*
> *mborajiú locro,*
> *tï torter,o*
> *sa botö,*
> *yurú guazú*

Which is Guarani for,

> Head like a big, fake chipá. (cheese bread)
> Body covered with warts.
> Eyes darting and cracking like the stew of a poor man.
> Button-eyes.
> Big mouth. . . .

And it is said and it is told that from that day on the alligator moves very slowly through the water. He is thinking and looking for an opportunity to take revenge on the monkey.

TELLING THIS STORY

Don't worry about including the Guarani chant if it intimidates you. Just do it in English. But it can be fun to try to share the Guarani, even though it is unlikely you will be able to pronounce it correctly.

PLAY WITH THIS STORY

Make an ugly yacaré. Draw a yacaré and make him as ugly as possible. Another option is to give the children a paper cutout of a yacaré. Provide bits of fabric, papers, and buttons and let them glue on items to make him grotesque.

Share Similar Stories

The Monkey and the Crocodile: A Jataka Tale from India by Paul Galdone (New York: Seabury, 1969).

Crocodile! Crocodile! by Barbara Baumgartner (London: Dorling Kindersley, 1994), pp. 8–12. In this story from India, the crocodile gives monkey a ride but wants to eat his heart.

The Rabbit's Escape by Suzanne Crowder Han (New York: Holt, 1999). In this Korean tale, the cuttlefish gives the rabbit a ride, wanting to eat his liver.

ABOUT THIS STORY

This story includes two motifs: K544 *Escape by alleged possession of external soul. Monkey caught for his heart (liver, etc.) as remedy makes his captor believe he has left his heart at home.* And K1241 *Trickster rides dupe horseback.* Paula Martín found eight Guarani versions of this story and one Toba version. The Guarani live in Paraguay and in adjacent parts of Argentina and Brazil.

THE NIGHT OF THE TATÚ

A Folktale of the Cashinahua People of Peru. For a Spanish text of this tale see Pachamama Tales, *pp. 177–178*

The Cashinahua people tell of a time long ago when there was no night at all. The sun shone hot and bright on and on and on. People were exhausted, with little chance to sleep.

But one day a woman noticed a little mouse scurrying into a hole at the base of her oven. She peeked in and saw the mouse curled up in the darkness there to sleep. "The mouse has its own night!" she exclaimed. "If only we could get a night like that."

Her son lay down by the oven and watched the mouse coming and going and then sleeping in its darkness. "I have an idea," he said. "Maybe we could ask the mouse to loan us his night. Let me try."

The boy saved the tastiest crumbs from his food that day, and he laid a trail of crumbs before the mouse's hole. When the mouse came out to investigate, the boy said, "If you like these crumbs, there is more for you. I will share with you every day if you will lend us your night."

The mouse gobbled up the delicious crumbs and nodded. Then from his eyes and ears a black fog began to rise to the sky. It covered the light of the sun. The sun fled from this fog and hurried down behind the horizon where it hid.

This was the first night for the people—the night of the mouse.

The people climbed into the hammocks hung under their thatch roofs and closed their eyes. They slept. So sweet. But almost immediately the sun was up again!

"The light of the mouse is too short!" the people complained. "We need a longer night."

Now that they knew that a night was possible, the hunters set out to find a longer night.

Deep in the forest they found a tapir, curled in a dark cave of leaves. "The tapir has found a night!" They caught the tapir and threatened it. "Lend us your night or we will have you for supper!"

The frightened tapir began to exude a dense smoke from its trunk, eyes, and whole body. The dark smoke rose to the sky and covered the sun. Quickly the sun rushed below the horizon to hide from this darkness.

This was the second night—the night of the tapir.

The hunters hurried home under the bright starlight. They had never seen the stars before and were amazed at the beauties of night. At home they built a campfire and were able to sit and talk in the darkness. Then they climbed into their hammocks and fell into such long and wonderful dreams. They dreamed and dreamed and dreamed. Days and days passed . . . weeks and weeks. Finally they began to awake.

"Oh no! We slept too long! Look at our village!"

Vines and weeds covered everything. Their houses were overrun with creepers, and their fields were covered with brush.

"This night was too long! We cannot use the night of the tapir."

Then the woman who had first noticed the mouse realized something. Her son, who was small, had found a short night. The men, who were large, had found a long night. Perhaps a woman could find a night that would be just right.

So the woman went out looking. She found Tatú, the armadillo, in his burrow. She could see that it was very dark in there. "Tatú, come out! I need to talk to you!"

Tatú woke up.

"Tatú, I would like to borrow your night. If you will loan it to the people, I will leave out my leftover food for you every day. Would you do that?"

Tatú thought. "I will. But you can only borrow it for one day."

"Agreed!" The woman stood back and waited. Tatú went back into his hole and stirred around.

Slowly a sweet darkness began to rise from Tatú's burrow. It spread slowly across the sky.

The sun gradually noticed and began to slip toward the horizon. But it did not flee quickly as before, and beautiful rays of color filled the sky as the sun retreated.

The people lit their fires, ate, and talked. Then they went to their hammocks. They slept well, but not too deeply. And after a few hours they awoke, rested and ready for work again.

This was the third night—the night of the Tatú. And this was a good night.

So the people did not return Tatú's night. They kept it for themselves.

That is why the poor little Tatú sleeps all day, but scurries around all night. He has no more night of his own to sleep in.

TELLING THIS STORY

This is a very magical story. Take your time with the images of the three different nights emerging and spreading across the sky and the people drifting into sleep.

PLAY WITH THIS STORY

Discuss the length of the night. Talk about the different lengths of night at different times of the year. What are the different lengths of night in different parts of the world? Decide which length you prefer. Show the world time zones on your laptop: http://24timezones.com. This map shows where the earth is currently in darkness and where it is in light. Where is dawn just breaking? Where is sunset arriving? Check the map later and see how night has fallen in some areas and sunshine arrived in others.

Share other stories telling how the time for night or sleep was established

"One Night's Sleep: A Coast Salish Folktale" in *Five Minute Tales* by Margaret Read MacDonald (Atlanta: August House, 2007). Bear wants to sleep five years at a time. Frog disagrees.

Crow and Fox and Other Animal Legends by Jan Thornhill (New York: Simon and Schuster, 1993), pp. 20–22. In this Native American story, the origin of night and day is caused by an argument between Grizzly Bear and Coyote.

Crocodile! Crocodile! Stories Told Around the World by Barbara Bamgartner (London: Dorling Kindersley, 1994), pp. 21–23. In this Native American story from the Allegheny River region, a chipmunk suggests the day be divided evenly, like stripes on a raccoon's tail, and the bear is unhappy.

When the World Was Young: Creation and Porquoi Tales by Margaret Mayo (New York: Simon and Schuster, 1996), pp. 49–53. In this Australian story from the Euahlayi people, Eagle bumps into Emu in the dark, breaks Emu's egg, and the yolk sets fire to the world. The animals can see the beauty of earth in the light, and daytime is created.

ABOUT THIS STORY

This is Motif A1172 *Determination of night and day*, Motif A1174 *Origin of night*, and Motif A1399.2.1 *Origin of sleep*. Paula Martín found four different versions of this sweet tale of the Cashinahua people. The Cashinahua live along the Curanja and Purus Rivers in the jungles of lowland eastern Peru and in adjacent areas of Brazil.

ABOUT THE AUTHOR

PAULA MARTÍN is a teacher, storyteller, and a specialist on children's and young adult's literature and on reading promotion. She was born in Buenos Aires Argentina. Her love for stories and folklore goes as far as her earliest years thanks to a grandfather that was always enthusiastic about telling the stories that came from his province of Tucumán and whose imagination knew no limits. Later on, in her journeys around South America, she continued gathering traditional stories from each one of the places that she visited. Her repertoire includes traditional and literary tales, poems, rhymes, riddles, tongue twisters, and songs, which she accompanies with Latin American instruments such as charango, quena, and sikus. Her interest in stories and folk music has taken her all around the countries in this collection.

As a bilingual storyteller, Paula has participated in several international festivals and has toured around the United States, Cuba, South Africa, United Kingdom, United Arab Emirates, Brazil, and Argentina.

She is a member of the organizing committee of the *Encuentro Internacional de Narración Oral* an international storytelling festival and conference that takes place every year at the Buenos

---

The Night of the Tatú

Aires Book Fair. In 2007, she received the *Premio Pregonero*, a prize that is awarded every year to people that promote children´s literature, issued by *Fundación El Libro*. She translated Dr. Margaret Read MacDonald's book *A Parent's Guide to Storytelling*, published as *Cuentos que van y vienen* (Buenos Aires, Aique Grupo Editor S. A., 2001), and *Desde los vientos de Manguito* by Elvia Pérez (Westport, CT: Libraries Unlimited, 2004), a book that received the American Folklore Society Aesop Prize in 2005.

At the present time, she works for the Plan Nacional de Lectura (National Reading Program) of the Ministerio de Educación de la Nación (National Educational Ministry) working with storytelling performances and teachers' workshops all over the country and is dedicated to promoting, teaching, and preserving storytelling. She is also immersed in the investigation, collection, and re-creation of world folktales, literary tales, and personal stories.

ABOUT THE EDITOR

Margaret Read MacDonald lived for two years in Buenos Aires and traveled throughout Chile, Paraguay, Uruguay, Bolivia, and Peru. She has returned to tell stories in Buenos Aires and Rio de Janeiro and has worked with Paula on several folktale and storytelling projects in the United States, Cuba, and Argentina.

THAILAND

From *Thai Tales: Folktales of Thailand* by Supaporn Vathanaprida. Edited by Margaret Read MacDonald (Libraries Unlimited, 1994).

THE ELEPHANT AND THE BEES

There was a time when elephants did not have long noses as they do now. In those days, elephants had to travel far to find their food. They never stayed at one place for long.

At this same time, there lived a swarm of bees that had built its hive on a low branch of a tree near the forest. Every day, those bees went out to collect honey from the flowers in the area.

One year, the weather became so dry that all the leaves dried up and fell from the trees. The poor elephants could not find anything to eat. Food was scarce. Vegetables and leaves could not grow because of the lack of water. Even the bees were starving.

Then one day a forest fire started and spread rapidly through the dry forest. The elephants ran away as fast as they could. But they could find no safe shelter. Closer and closer came the fire. Then the elephants saw the bees buzzing ahead of them. Perhaps these flying insects could help them. When the bees realized that the huge elephants were asking *them* for aid, they laughed. Then they said, "Yes, we can tell you about a safe shelter from the fire. But you must help us in return."

The elephants agreed. To their surprise, the bees asked the elephants to open their huge mouths. Then the bees flew right inside the elephants' noses. They *stayed* there. From this safe hiding place, the bees directed the elephants. They guided them to a large pond. "Go right into the middle of the pond. Do not move until the fire has passed on."

The elephants did just as the bees suggested. Standing in the pond for several days, they waited until the fire had burned itself out. All the trees of the forest were burnt away. But the elephants and the bees had survived.

Now the elephants emerged from the pond and called to the bees to come on out of their noses and mouths.

But the bees liked living in that spot. They refused to come out! Those elephants were so angry. *"Prae Praen! Prae Praen!"* they trumpeted. They shook their heavy heads from side to side. They blew hard on their noses. Harder and harder they blew, trying to blow those bees out. And the harder they blew, the longer their noses became! But the bees would not come out. And all of their blowing and trumpeting served only to make their poor noses very, very long.

Now the elephants decided they could rid themselves of those pesky bees with fire. After all, the bees had flown into the elephants' noses and mouths in the first place in order to escape fire. So lighting a fire, the elephants began to inhale the smoke. Opening their mouths, they breathed deeply, then shut their mouths tightly and held that smoke inside. It worked. The bees could not stand that smoke. They flew hurriedly from the noses of the elephants.

But now that the bees had become accustomed to living in such a warm, dark hole, they looked for a similar place to live. Since then these bees build their homes only in hollow trees. They are called *Phung Phrong* bees, which means "the hole like an elephant's mouth." But to get their honeycombs is easy: you simply smoke them out. They are still afraid of fire!

As for the elephants, they were glad to be rid of those bees. But they feared another infestation, so to make sure their noses and mouths were kept free of bees, they began to swallow water and blow it out through their noses. To this day they keep that habit. And it is a very good technique, too, for making sure your nose is free of bees!

TELLING THIS STORY

When I tell this story now, I have the bees fly to the east, west, and north looking for escape. At each place, they cry, "Fai Mai!" Which means "Fire!" in Thai. Then they fly to the south and find water. When my Thai friend Dr. Wajuppa Tossa tells this story, she ends by saying, "If you see an elephant in the zoo blowing water out of his nose, just tell him, 'Don't worry, Mr. Elephant. The bees are all gone. The bees are all gone.'" She asks her students to each pat another student on the shoulder and say this to them. It makes for a very sweet ending moment for the story.

PLAY WITH THIS STORY

Act it out. Divide the children into teams: bees and elephants. Tell the story again and let each group repeat their parts and act them out with you. There will be lots of buzzing and trumpeting.

Break the children into teams and let them act out the story. One is the elephant. One is the bee.

Compare to Another Story

Read aloud Rudyard Kipling's "How the Elephant Got His Trunk," found in his *Just So Stories*. This is not a folktale. Kipling made up the story.

Write your own story. Create your own story of how the elephant may have gotten his trunk.

ABOUT THIS STORY

Motif A2334.3 *Origin and nature of animal's proboscis.* B481.3 *Helpful bees.*

For another tellable version of this story, see *Teaching with Story: Classroom Connections to Storytelling* by Margaret Read MacDonald, Jennifer MacDonald Whitman, and Nathaniel Forest Whitman (August House, 2013), pp. 92–94.

THE GOOD BOY

To be respectful of elders is a valued character trait in Thailand. One should always pay respect to one's elder, either in age or in status. One usually calls all elders by a respectful title such as Uncle (Lung), *or Aunt* (Pa), *or Grandfather* (Ta), *or Grandmother* (Yai), *even though they are not actually relatives.*

In Thailand, in the olden days, elephants played an important role in life. Elephants were used as trucks and tractors in forestry. They pulled logs from high mountains, dragging them down to the riverbanks. Elephants were also used as fighting tanks in war. Wild elephants were rounded up and brought to a training school, where they were trained to be either working elephants or fighting elephants. Albino elephants or "white elephants" were considered rare and sacred. Any king who owned a white elephant was considered great. Today, elephants are still used in the timber industry in northern Thailand.

Once there was a boy whose parents were very poor. Still, they were good parents. They taught the boy to be obedient and considerate. They taught him to be respectful of all elders, regardless of their social status or wealth. This child was a good boy. He followed the ways his parents had taught him.

One day, when the boy was searching for wood in the forest, he became lost. He felt very frightened, but he tried to look for signs which might show him the way back to his home. As he searched this way and that, the boy suddenly came face to face with a huge, full-grown elephant that was strolling through the forest munching on bamboo and wild bananas. The boy was terrified at the sight of this huge animal, but he remembered his parents' admonitions to respect great age. This elephant was so large that it must be very old indeed. Trembling, the boy knelt and bowed three times in respect to the great elephant.

Seeing this, the elephant was surprised. He came closer to the boy and asked, "Young boy, why do you show respect to me?"

The boy answered, "Dear Elephant the Mighty One, I bow down because you are strong. I bow down because you are my elder. My parents taught me to pay respect to all who deserve respect. I believe you are one of those; therefore, I pay homage to you."

"You are a good boy," said the elephant. "You follow your elders' instructions. I will reward your good conduct. This bell was given to me by the King of the Elephants. I now give it to you. If ever you are in danger or in need of help, you should ring this bell. Any elephants who are nearby will come at once to your rescue."

The boy gratefully accepted the bell. He thanked the elephant. Then the elephant showed the boy the way back to his village. "Follow this path and it will lead to your home. I must leave now." The elephant turned, and disappeared into the deep forest.

The boy followed the elephant's advice and soon reached his home. He told his parents about the encounter with the elephant. They were pleased that their son had received this gift from the elephant. All this because he was such a good boy, doing exactly what his parents had taught him.

Several months later, the boy and his father went back into the forest to gather firewood. They planned to make charcoal to sell on New Year's Day. They left home early in the morning, and the father worked to cut branches from a large tree. Suddenly, a storm came up. The boy and his father took refuge in the crevice of a large rock, but the tree on which the father had been cutting broke in half in the wind. The tree fell right across the crevice, trapping the boy and his father. They were unhurt, but unable to escape. They called for help, but so deep in the forest, there was no one to hear.

For several hours, they huddled in the rock crevice, then the boy remembered his gift, the elephant bell. He pulled out the bell and began to ring it. Soon the boy and his father heard a crashing sound, as several elephants came lumbering through the forest. Wrapping their strong trunks around the tree, the elephants lifted it from the rock, and the trapped boy and his father were freed. Gratefully, the boy bowed before the elephants and thanked them. It was as his friend, the elephant, had said. Help had come immediately.

Meanwhile his elephant friend had fallen on bad luck. He had been captured and imprisoned in the city where he was being trained as a fighting elephant. His huge size made him a fierce fighter, but his wild temperament did not allow him to adapt to this life. Eventually, he went mad. The wild elephant killed his trainers and escaped into the jungle. From there he would emerge, raging, to devastate villages. Elephant trainers were sent to capture him, but they returned injured and the elephant's reign of terror continued.

When the boy heard of this wild elephant, he volunteered at once to try to capture it. His parents begged him not to undertake such a dangerous task, but the boy showed them his bell and assured them that this bell would help him accomplish the risky mission.

The boy hurried to the king's palace and volunteered his services. The king's soldiers escorted the boy to the area where the wild elephant was currently raging, but as soon as the elephant emerged from the forest, those soldiers ran for their lives, leaving the boy standing alone.

The elephant bellowed and prepared to attack. The boy calmly spread a cloth on the ground. There, he bowed three times to the enraged beast, ringing his bell all the while.

Suddenly, the elephant stopped. It heard the bell, and it remembered. The elephant walked slowly to the boy and laid its trunk on top of the boy's head to greet him.

Talking softly to the elephant, the boy reassured it. He persuaded it to go back to town with him. And the huge elephant calmly walked beside the boy back to the king's palace.

The king was very pleased. He rewarded the boy and appointed him head of the elephant troop. This boy was a good boy. With this excellent job, he took fine care of his parents when they grew old.

PLAY WITH THIS STORY

Play a raging-elephant game. Have the children stand in a circle. One child is in the center. The elephants in the circle all rage and trumpet and stomp around. The child in the center rings a little bell, and all of the elephants calm down and lower their trunks and bow to this child. Repeat with other children taking the roll of the bell ringer.

Compare to Similar Stories

Androcles and the Lion by Dennis Noland (New York: Harcourt, 1997). In this story, a boy removes a thorn from a lion's paw, and the lion later rewards him.

Androcles and the Lion by Janet Stevens (New York: Holiday House, 1989).

St. Jerome and the Lion by Margaret Hodges, illustrated by Barry Moser (New York: Orchard, 1991).

Misoso by Verna Aardema (New York, Knopf, 1994), pp. 79–87. In this Nigerian tale, a man removes a thorn from an ape's foot, and the ape rescues the man's stolen son.

ABOUT THIS STORY

B381 *Androcles and the Lion.* D1213 *Magic bell.* B443.3 *Helpful elephant.*

A story is also told of the Lord Buddha in which he gently stands in the path of a raging elephant and calms it. See "Nalagiri the Elephant" in *The Hungry Tigress: Buddhist Legends & Tales* by Rafe Martin (Berkeley, CA: Parallax Press, 1990), pp. 30–35.

A Note from the Storyteller

How I heard the stories: My mother was a teacher so she had to go to work every day so my great-grandmother acted as my nanny. She would play with me and look after me during the day. She always said, "Little one, if you behave well today I'll tell you a story at bedtime." Naturally I was an exceptionally well-behaved child! Every night she would tell me stories—some from her own imagination, some from her reading materials, and many from what she heard at the monastery. These are usually the Jataka tales told by the monks. They were one of my happiest moments. Growing up, whenever I came across some difficulties, I kept remembering the lessons I learned from those stories—such as patience, respect, diligence, honesty, humility, and so on.

Being a devout Buddhist, my great-grandmother stayed overnight at the monastery on Buddhist days. In the morning, she would offer food to the monks and then listen to their teachings and chanting. The monks usually taught by citing stories from the Lord Buddha's many lives, the Jataka tales.

ABOUT THE STORYTELLER

SUPAPORN VATHANAPRIDA, a librarian with the King County Library System in Seattle, is a first-generation immigrant from Thailand. Since living in the United States, Su keeps thinking back to the happy time when her great-grandmother told her bedtime stories. Some are just fun to listen to, but many are life lessons. They show her how to deal with difficulties in everyday living. In addition to this book, Su is author of the Thai text of *The Girl Who Wore Too Much* by Margaret Read MacDonald (Little Rock: August House, 2005. Su share her stories and speaks about Thai culture at schools in the Seattle area

ABOUT THE EDITOR

Margaret Read MacDonald worked beside Supaporn Vathanaprida for many years at the Bothell Regional Library in Bothell, Washington. When Dr. MacDonald completed her *Storyteller's Sourcebook*, an index to children's folktales from around the world, Su was incensed that there were not more Thai folktales included. So Margaret told Su to go write a book of Thai tales. Remembering the stories her grandmother had told her as a child…she did!

UKRAINE

From *The Magic Egg and Other Tales from Ukraine* by Barbara J. Suwyn. Edited by Natalie O. Kononenko (Libraries Unlimited, 1997).

THE CHRISTMAS SPIDERS

Retold by Natalie O. Kononenko.

Once there was a poor peasant family. They were so poor that they had almost nothing at all. The children wore tattered clothing and ran around barefoot, even in winter. Many, many times there was not enough to eat and they all went to bed hungry. Through the seasons they somehow managed to survive, but one year was especially difficult. The summer was hot and windy, and the little patch of dirt they called their garden dried up. Fall came, then winter. Christmas was on its way.

As the holiday season approached, the parents talked to one another. They wanted to make the day special for their children, and more than anything they wanted to give the little ones a treat to celebrate Christmas. But how could they? They had no money. They could not even afford warm clothes or shoes for the children. No, there would be no gifts.

"Let's at least put up a Christmas tree," said the father. "Maybe if we have faith, everything will work out. Maybe I'll find work and we can buy some candy and nuts to put on the tree. Then we could let the children have them as their presents on Christmas morning."

The father grew excited and happy as he spoke, but the mother shook her head sadly. "Don't get their hopes up," she said. "A tree will only remind the children that we have nothing. You know they'll be getting no presents. It's better not to disappoint them."

The father's smile quickly faded. "Maybe you're right," he conceded.

Days passed, and the snow piled high outside the door. The closer they came to Christmas, the more anxious the father became. Finally he decided the family could not celebrate the holiday without a tree. Taking his ax in hand, he ventured out into the snow toward the forest. He walked and walked, his breath clouding before him in little puffs. When he reached a clearing, he saw that there in the middle of it stood a small, perfect tree.

"This tree was meant to be ours!" the man exclaimed and excitedly he chopped it down. Then he loaded the tree on his shoulder and carried it home.

When he arrived, the children met him at the door.

"Daddy, Daddy," they cried, clapping their hands, "does this mean we're going to have Christmas after all?"

"Well, I suppose so," the father mumbled sheepishly. But when the mother heard this, she ran to the kitchen to hide her tears in her apron. Her husband followed her.

"Now, now," he said, taking her gently by the shoulders, "we will have a Christmas. Surely we can find a few coins around here."

So together they scoured the house, searching for a few pennies to buy presents with. First they checked the money box. It was empty. Then they looked into all the secret places where they might have hidden money, or where a stray coin might have fallen. But everywhere they looked they found nothing.

Finally the father said, "There is not a cent in this house. I will go into town to see if I can find work. Maybe someone will hire me to chop wood or carry coal. I am strong and there are many that need help. Maybe I can earn a little change to buy Christmas presents for our family." The wife said nothing, but sighed and nodded in agreement.

The next day the father went to town, asking for work, but it was too close to the holiday. Everyone was busy with Christmas preparations, and no one was thinking about routine tasks. Even if they had been, money was tight at holiday time. Again and again the man was rejected.

While the father searched for work, the little Christmas tree stood alone in the corner. No one decorated it. No one admired it. No one even gave it a second thought. In the silence of the little house's dark corner, tiny spiders moved into the tree, one by one, spinning their webs on this branch and that, from one branch to another.

Then Christmas Eve came. As night fell, the father became cold and discouraged. He gave up looking for work and trudged home. When he entered the house, he saw that the tree was filled with spider webs. His mouth dropped.

"Our tree has been infested with spiders," he gasped. "Clean it up at once! We can't have bugs in our home."

The family came running and gathered around the tree. They too stared open-mouthed, for it was indeed covered with webs.

"But Daddy," piped up Oksana, the youngest daughter, "aren't spiders God's creatures too? Look how beautiful their webs are! Can't we leave them on for one day as Christmas decorations?"

The other children chimed in, begging and pleading, so the father and mother agreed to leave the tree as it was for the night. Then the whole family went to bed.

The next morning the children awoke early and ran to the tree. The mother and father were still in bed, but they heard the children pattering about.

"Poor darlings," said the mother. "I told you they would expect something."

"Yes," agreed the father, "I guess you are right." He had no sooner said the words than they heard the cries of little Oksana.

"Mommy! Daddy! Come quick! Come and look at the tree! The spider webs are even more beautiful today!"

The mother and father roused themselves from bed and hurried to where the tree stood. As they approached, they saw the spider webs glistening in a strange, vivid way. They touched the webs. They were hard! Then the father reached for one.

"They're silver!" he marveled, turning the web over in his hand. 'In the night they turned to silver!"

The children clapped and jumped up and down. "Thank you! Thank you for our Christmas present," they all cried. Their mother hugged them all and smiled through her tears.

That Christmas turned out to be the most wonderful Christmas of all. The parents took the webs from the tree and sold them. They bought their family food, warm clothes, shoes, and even warm boots for winter. Together they gave great thanks for the blessings of God's creatures.

That is why we do not kill spiders anymore, and why many will not even sweep their webs from their houses. For it is true—Even the lowliest creature on earth is a gift from above.

PLAY WITH THIS STORY

Make spider web decorations. Place pins in a piece of cardboard and weave a lightweight white string around them to create your spider web. Spray starch the string and leave it to dry.

ABOUT THIS STORY

Spider webs form a magical element in many stories. A spider is said to have woven a web across the entrance to the cave to make soldiers pursuing the Baby Jesus believe that there was no one hiding inside. (*The Cobweb Curtain* by Jenny Koralek (New York: Holt, 1989)). And the spider is said to have spun a web across a cave entrance to persuade pursuers of Mohammed that no one was hiding inside. (*Somone Saw a Spider* by Shirley Climo (New York: Crowell, 1985) pp. 57–62); "The Miracle of the Spider Web" in *Tales from the Arabian Peninsula* by Margaret Read MacDonald and Nadia Jameel Taibah (Westport, CT; Libraries Unlimited, 2015).

Motif B523.1 *Spider-web over hole saves fugitive.*

Stith-Thompson cites variants of this motif from Turkey, Jewish tradition, Lapland, India, Japan, and Africa's Fang people. El-Shamy cites an Egyptian variant. MacDonald cites Indonesian and Jewish variants. MacDonald and Sturm cite an Arabian version and a variant in which the spider hides Mary and Joseph and the Baby Jesus. Type 967 *The Man Saved by a Spider Web* includes variants from Catalonia, England, the Netherlands, and the United States.

In a Spanish tale, the Virgin Mary makes a lace mantilla of spider webs. (*The Way of the Storyteller* by Ruth Sawyer (New York: Viking, 1962), pp. 229–236.)

THE LITTLE ROUND BUN

There once lived an old farmer and his wife, who were so poor they didn't know what to do. They were too old to work, and each day they grew poorer, sadder, and hungrier, until one day there was no more food left in the house.

"Why don't you bake us some bread, old woman?" said the farmer.

"Because we have no flour," replied his wife.

"Can't you find even a little?" asked the old man.

So the old woman scraped out the very last bits from the flour bin and added a few dry crumbs and got just enough to make a little round bun, or a *kalach*, as they say in Ukraine. She found two dried-up currants and a leathery strip of apple peel and these she pressed into the dough so that they looked like two little black eyes and a crooked little smile. The old woman popped the bun into the oven. She was so proud of herself that she began to sweep the hut and hum, beaming brightly as she worked. As the little bun cooked, the house filled with the smell of baking bread, and the old man began smiling too.

When the old woman pulled the *kalach* from the oven, it was so perfect that she and the old man both gasped, "Ahhh!" She set the bun on the windowsill, and the two of them waited eagerly for it to cool.

Suddenly the *kalach* jumped from the windowsill down to the ground. There it started rolling down the road. The old couple jumped up from their chairs and chased after it, waving their arms wildly and shouting, but the *kalach* kept rolling. As it rolled, the little bun sang:

> I'm a little round bun straight from the oven
> And I roll all day beneath the golden sun.
> If you want to catch me, you can run, run, run,
> But I'll just roll away, 'cause I'm a little round bun.

The old man and old woman ran and ran, but the bun rolled much faster than they could run and eventually they gave up and went back home. The little bun kept rolling down the road. By and by it met a rabbit.

The rabbit took one look at the *kalach* and it said, "What a tasty meal has rolled my way!" But just as he started to reach for the bun, the little *kalach* spoke.

"Don't eat me yet," said the bun. "Wait till I sing my little song." So the rabbit sat back on his haunches while the little round bun sang:

I'm a little round bun straight from the oven
And I roll all day beneath the golden sun.
I rolled from the farmer and I rolled from his wife,
And I'll roll from you for my life, life, life.
If you want to catch me, you can run, run, run,
But I'll just roll away, 'cause I'm a little round bun.

As it sang, the little round bun rocked to and fro. When it reached the end of the song, it quickly rolled away. The rabbit hopped after the bun, but the little *kalach* rolled very fast. It wasn't long before the rabbit tired of the chase and gave up. The little round bun rolled on and on.

By and by the *kalach* ran into a lean and hungry wolf.

"Aha!" said the wolf. "That bun looks like a tender bite." Drooling, he reached for it, but when he did, the bun spoke.

"Don't eat me yet, Mr. Wolf. Listen to my little song first."

"Hmm," thought the wolf. "I do like music." So he lay down on the road and closed his eyes while the little bun sang:

I'm a little round bun straight from the oven
And I roll all day beneath the golden sun.
I rolled from the farmer and I rolled from his wife,
And I rolled from the rabbit for my life, life, life.
If you want to catch me, you can run, run, run,
But I'll just roll away, 'cause I'm a little round bun.

Again the little bun rocked to and fro as it sang, and when it reached the end of the song, it quickly rolled away. The wolf opened his eyes and saw what was happening, and he jumped up and began chasing the *kalach*. But the little round bun rolled faster and faster down the road, and soon the wolf could not even see it. Panting, he turned around and went home.

The little round bun rolled on. By and by the little round bun ran into a huge brown bear. The bear was busy picking blackberries, but when he saw the little bun, he dropped the berries and swung a mighty paw toward it. The little bun managed to dodge the bear's paw, and, shaking with fear, it cried out, "Please don't eat me yet. Wait till I sing my little song."

"Oh, who cares about your stupid song," grumbled the bear, but he groaned and sat down to listen to the little bun sing.

I'm a little round bun straight from the oven
And I roll all day beneath the golden sun.
I rolled from the farmer and I rolled from his wife,
And I rolled from the rabbit for my life, life, life.
I rolled from the wolf—I rolled right away,
'Cause I'm a little round bun and I'm made that way.

If you want to catch me, you can run, run, run,
But I'll just roll away, 'cause I'm a little round bun.

Rocking to and fro, the *kalach* sang and sang. When it reached the end of its ditty, it quickly rolled away.

"Hey, wait!" roared the bear, and he staggered to his feet. But it was too late. The little round bun was rolling down the road as fast as the wind, and the old bear could not catch up. Finally the bear gave up and went back to the blackberry patch. And the little round bun rolled on.

By and by the *kalach* ran into a sleek red fox.

"You look just like my dinner," said the fox, but as she reached for the bun, it spoke up once again.

"Please don't eat me yet," it begged. "Wait till you hear my little song."

So the fox sat down and arranged her fluffy tail around her. Then she perked up her ears while the little bun sang:

I'm a little round bun straight from the oven
And I roll all day beneath the golden sun.
I rolled from the farmer and I rolled from his wife,
And I rolled from the rabbit for my life, life, life.
I rolled from the wolf—I rolled right away,
And I rolled from the bear, 'cause I'm made that way.
If you want to catch me, you can run, run, run,
But I'll just roll away, 'cause I'm a little round bun.

As it sang, the little bun rocked to and fro. When it reached the end, it started to roll away, but the fox called after it, saying, "Oh, please don't go—your song is so lovely. Sing it for me again, but this time come closer, so I can hear it better."

The little round bun grinned and rolled up so close to the fox that it could feel her breath. The fox closed her eyes and sighed blissfully as the little bun sang:

I'm a little round bun straight from the oven
And I roll all day beneath the golden sun.
I rolled from the farmer and I rolled from his wife,
And I rolled from the rabbit for my life, life, life.
I rolled from the wolf—I rolled right away,
And I rolled from the bear, 'cause I'm made that way.
If you want to catch me, you can run, run, run,
But I'll just roll away, 'cause I'm a little round bun.

When the *kalach* finished, the fox clapped and cried," "Bravo, bravo!" The little round bun smiled its crooked smile. Then the sleek red fox begged, "Oh your song is so lovely! Can I hear it just one more time? Please? If you sit on my nose and sing, I'll be able to hear it very well."

So the little *kalach* jumped onto the fox's nose and began to sing: "I'm a little round bun straight from the oven," it began, rocking to and fro, "and I roll all day beneath the golden—." SNAP! The fox opened her mouth, clamped her jaws around the little round bun, and gobbled it right up. Then she licked her lips, smiled, and sauntered down the road, singing:

There was a little round bun who came straight from the oven
And it rolled all day beneath the golden sun.
If you want to catch a meal, you can run, run, run,
But it's your wits that will get you a little round bun.

PLAY WITH THIS STORY

Act it out. Add several children for each animal the bun meets so all can participate. An adult could act the roll of the fox.

Compare to Similar Stories

The Gingerbread Boy by Paul Galone (New York: Seabury, 1975).
The Gingerbread Man by William Curtis Holdsworth (New York: Farrar, Straus and Giroux, 1968).
Johnny Cake by Joseph Jacobs (New York: Putnam, 1933).
Johny Cake Ho by Ruth Sawyer, illustrated by Robert McCloskey (New York: Viking, 1956).
Also find a fun Dutch version in which a pig catches the pancake: *Legends and Folk Tales of Holland* by De Leeuw (New York: Nelson, 1963), pp. 89–91.
And see "The Winged, Hairy, and Buttery Friends" on page 135 for a Russian version of this tale.

ABOUT THIS STORY

Motif Z33.1 *The fleeing pancake. A woman makes a pancake which flees. Various animals try in vain to stop it. Finally the fox eats it up.* Type 2025.

This is a popular tale throughout Europe. MacDonald's *Storyteller's Sourcebook* cites sources from England, Ireland, the Netherlands, Russia, Scotland, and the United States. MacDonald and Sturm's *Storyteller's Sourcebook* adds more British sources and a Norwegian version: *The Pancake Boy: An Old Norwegian Folk Tale* by Lorinda Bryan Cauley (New York: Putnam, 1988).

ABOUT THE AUTHORS

BARBARA J. SUWYN is an author, editor, poet, and a lover of story. Her interest in Ukrainian folklore was first ignited by researching the library of her former employer, Dr. Bohdan S. Wynar. Her interest grew through subsequent correspondence and story sharing with editor Dr. Natalie Kononenko. Her book *The Magic Egg and Other Tales from Ukraine* (Libraries Unlimited, 1997) represents a profound respect for the deep cultural heritage of Ukraine. She currently lives in Denver, Colorado.

NATALIE O. KONONENKO, Associate Professor at the University of Virginia, learned many of the Ukrainian tales in *The Magic Egg* from her mother and grandfather.

Photo my Mary Taber

ABOUT THE TALE NOTES

Motif and tale type indexes are referenced in the tale notes.

Motif numbers are from:

Stith Thompson, *Motif-Index of Folk-Literature*. 6 vols. Bloomington, IN: Indiana University Press, 1966.

Motif numbers noted as "MacDonald" or "MacDonald and Sturm" are from:

Margaret Read MacDonald, *The Storyteller's Sourcebook: A Subject, Title, and Motif-Index to Folklore Collections for Children*. Detroit: Neal-Schuman/Gale Research, 1982.

Margaret Read MacDonald and Brian W. Sturm. *The Storyteller's Sourcebook: A Subject, Title, and Motif-Index to Folklore Collections for Children: 1983–1999*. Farmington Hills, MI: Gale Group, 2000.

Type numbers are from:

Antti Aarne and Stith Thompson. *The Types of the Folktale*. Helsinki: Folklore Fellows Communications, 1961.

Libraries Unlimited World Folklore Series

Visit www.abc-clio.com for more details on these exciting titles.

*Tales from starred items are included in this *Storyteller's Sampler.*

***Arabian Peninsula:** Tales from the Arabian Peninsula* by Nadia Jameel Taibah and Margaret Read MacDonald (Libraries Unlimited, 2015).

***Armenia:** The Flower of Paradise and Other Armenian Tales* by Bonnie C. Marshall. Edited by Virginia Tashjian (Libraries Unlimited, 2007).

***Australian Aboriginal:** Gadi Mirrabooka: Australian Aboriginal Tales from the Dreaming*. Retold by Pauline E. McLeod, Francis Firebrace Jones, and June E. Barker. Edited by Helen F. McKay (Libraries Unlimited, 2001).

***Balkans:** Tales from the Heart of the Balkans*. Retold by Bonnie C. Marshall (Libraries Unlimited, 2001).

***Brazil:** Brazilian Folktales* by Livia de Almeida and Ana Portella. Edited by Margaret Read MacDonald. (Libraries Unlimited, 2006).

Bushmen: *Why Ostriches Don't Fly and Other Tales from the African Bush* by I. Murphy Lewis (Libraries Unlimited, 1997).

Celtic: *The Celtic Breeze: Stories of the Otherworld from Scotland, Ireland, and Wales* by Heather McNeil (Libraries Unlimited, 2002).

China: *The Magic Lotus Lantern and Other Tales from the Han Chinese* by Haiwang Yuan (Libraries Unlimited, 2006).

China: *Princess Peacock: Tales from the Other Peoples of China.* Retold by Haiwang Yuan (Libraries Unlimited, 2008).

*Cuba: *From the Winds of Manguito: Cuban Folktales in English and Spanish. Desde los Vientos de Manguito: Cuentos folklóricos de Cuba, en inglés y español* by Elvia Pérez. Translated by Paula Martín. Edited by Margaret Read MacDonald. (Libraries Unlimited, 2004).

England: *English Folktales.* Edited by Dan Keding and Amy Douglas (Libraries Unlimited, 2005).

*Finland: *The Enchanted Wood and Other Tales from Finland* by Norma J. Livo and George O. Livo (Libraries Unlimited, 1999).

Germany: *The Seven Swabians, and other German Folktales* by Anna E. Altmann (Libraries Unlimited, 2006).

*Greece: *Folktales from Greece: A Treasury of Delights.* Retold by Soula Mitakidou and Anthony L. Manna, with Melpomeni Kanatsouli (Libraries Unlimited, 2002).

*Haiti: *When Night Falls, Kric! Crac! Haitian Folktales* by Liliane Nérette Louis. Edited by Fred Hay (Libraries Unlimited, 1999).

*Hmong: *Folk Stories of the Hmong: Peoples of Laos, Thailand, and Vietnam* by Norma J. Livo and Dia Cha (Libraries Unlimited, 1991).

*India: *Jasmine and Coconuts: South Indian Tales* by Cathy Spagnoli and Paramasivam Samanna (Libraries Unlimited, 1999).

*Indonesia: *Indonesian Folktales* by Murti Bunanta. Edited by Margaret Read MacDonald. (Libraries Unlimited, 2003).

*Japan: *Folktales from the Japanese Countryside* by Hiroko Fujita. Edited by Fran Stallings (Libraries Unlimited, 2008).

*Kenya: *Hyena and the Moon: Stories to Tell from Kenya* by Heather McNeil (Libraries Unlimited, 1994).

*Korea: *A Tiger by the Tail and Other Stories from the Heart of Korea.* Retold by Lindy Soon Curry. Edited by Chan-eung Park (Libraries Unlimited, 1999).

*Kurdish: *A Fire in My Heart: Kurdish Tales.* Retold by Diane Edgecomb. With contributions by Mohammed M. A. Ahmed and Cheto Ozel (Libraries Unlimited, 2008).

*Laos: *Lao Folktales* by Wajuppa Tossa with Kongdeuan Nettavong. Edited by Margaret Read MacDonald (Libraries Unlimited, 2008).

*Malaysia, Singapore, Brunei: *The Singing Top: Tales from Malaysia, Singapore, and Brunei* by Margaret Read MacDonald (Libraries Unlimited, 2008).

*Mayan: *Mayan Folktales: Cuentos folklóricos mayas.* Retold and edited by Susan Conklin Thompson, Keith Steven Thompson, and Lidia López de López (Libraries Unlmited, 2007).

*Mexico: *The Eagle on the Cactus: Traditional Stories from Mexico.* Retold by Angel Vigil (Libraries Unlimited, 2000).

Mexico: *The Corn Woman: Stories and Legends of the Hispanic Southwest. La Mujer del Maíz: Cuentos y Leyendas del Sudoeste Hispano.* Retold by Angel Vigil (Libraries Unlimited, 1994).

*Mongolia: *Mongolian Folktales.* Retold by Dashdondog Jamba and Borolzoi Dashdondog. Edited by Anne Pellowski (Libraries Unlimited, 2009).

*Nepal: *From the Mango Tree and Other Folktales from Nepal* by Kavita Ram Shrestha and Sarah Lamstein (Libraries Unlimited, 1997).

*Netherlands: *The Flying Dutchman and Other Folktales from the Netherlands* by Theo Meder (Libraries Unlimited, 2008).

Pennsylvania Dutch: *In Days Gone By: Folklore and Traditions of the Pennsylvania Dutch* by Audrey Burie Kirchner and Margaret R. Tassia (Libraries Unlimited, 1996).

*Philippines: *Tales from the 7,000 Isles: Filipino Folk Stories* by Dianne de las Casas and Zarah C. Gagatiga (Libraries Unlimited, 2011).

*Poland: *Polish Folktales and Folklore.* Retold by Michal Malinowski and Anne Pellowski (Libraries Unlimited, 2009).

*Russia: *The Snow Maiden and other Russian Tales.* Translated and Retold by Bonnie C. Marshall (Libraries Unlimited, 2004).

*Siberia: *Far North Tales: Stories from the Peoples of the Arctic Circle.* Translated and retold by Bonnie C. Marshall. Edited by Kira Van Deusen (Libraries Unlimited, 2011).

*South America: *Pachamama Tales: Folklore from Argentina, Bolivia, Chile, Paraguay, Peru, and Uruguay.* Retold and translated by Paula Martín. Edited by Margaret Read MacDonald (Libraries Unlimited, 2014).

Taiwan: *Tales from the Taiwanese.* Retold by Gary Marvin Davison (Libraries Unlimited, 2004).

*Thailand: *Thai Tales: Folktales of Thailand* by Supaporn Vathanaprida. Edited by Margaret Read MacDonald (Libraries Unlimited, 1994).

Tlingit: *Images of a People: Tlingit Myths and Legends* by Mary Helen Pelton and Jacquiline DiGennaro (Libraries Unlimited, 1992).

*Ukraine: *The Magic Egg and Other Tales from Ukraine* by Barbara J. Suwyn (Libraries Unlimited, 1997).

LIBRARIES UNLIMITED WORLD FOLKLORE SERIES

Visit www.abc-clio.com for more details on these exciting titles.

Folk Stories of the Hmong: Peoples of Laos, Thailand, and Vietnam
Norma J. Livo and Dia Cha

Images of a People: Tlingit Myths and Legends
Mary Pelton and Jaquelle DiGennaro

Hyena and the Moon: Stories to Tell from Kenya
Heather McNeil

Thai Tales: Folktales of Thailand
Retold by Supaporn Vathanaprida, Edited by Margaret Read MacDonald

The Corn Woman: Stories and Legends of the Hispanic Southwest
Angel Vigil

From the Mango Tree and Other Folktales from Nepal
Kavita Ram Shrestha and Sarah Lamstein

Why Ostriches Don't Fly and Other Tales from the African Bush
Irene Lewis

The Magic Egg and Other Tales from Ukraine
Retold by Barbara J. Suwyn, Edited by Natalie O. Kononenko

Jasmine and Coconuts: South Indian Tales
Cathy Spagnoli and Paramasivam Samanna

When Night Falls, Kric! Krac! Haitian Folktales
Liliane Nérette Louis, Edited by Fred J. Hay

The Enchanted Wood and Other Tales from Finland
Norma J. Livo and George O. Livo

A Tiger by the Tail and Other Stories from the Heart of Korea
Retold by Lindy Soon Curry, Edited by Chan-Eun Park

The Eagle on the Cactus: Traditional Stories from Mexico
Angel Vigil

Tales from the Heart of the Balkans
Retold by Bonnie C. Marshall, Edited by Vasa D. Mihailovich

The Celtic Breeze: Stories of the Otherworld from Scotland, Ireland, and Wales
Heather McNeil

Gadi Mirrabooka: Australian Aboriginal Tales from the Dreaming
Retold by Pauline E. McLeod, Francis Firebreace Jones, and June E. Parker, Edited by Helen F. McKay

Folktales from Greece: A Treasury of Delights
Retold by Soula Mitakidou and Anthony L. Manna, with Melpomeni Manatsouli

Indonesian Folktales
Retold by Murti Bunanta, Edited by Margaret Read MacDonald

Tales from the Taiwanese
Retold by Gary Marvin Davison

From the Winds of Manguito, Desde los vientos de Manguito: Cuban Folktales in English and Spanish, Cuentos folklóricos de Cuba, en inglés y español
Retold by Elvia Pérez, Translated by Paula Martín, Edited by Margaret Read MacDonald

The Snow Maiden and Other Russian Tales
Translated and Retold by Bonnie C. Marshall

English Folktales
Edited by Dan Keding and Amy Douglas

The Seven Swabians, and Other German Folktales
Anna E. Altmann

Brazilian Folktales
Livia de Almeida and Ana Portella, Edited by Margaret Read MacDonald

The Magic Lotus Lantern and Other Tales from the Han Chinese
Haiwang Yuan

The Flower of Paradise and Other Armenian Tales
Translated and Retold by Bonnie C. Marshall, Edited and with a Foreword by Virginia Tashjian

Mayan Folktales, Cuentos folklóricos mayas
Retold and Edited by Susan Conklin Thompson, Keith Thompson, and Lidia López de López

The Flying Dutchman and Other Folktales from the Netherlands
Theo Meder

Folktales from the Japanese Countryside
As Told by Hiroko Fujita, Edited by Fran Stallings with Harold Wright and Miki Sakurai

A Fire in My Heart: Kurdish Tales
Retold by Diane Edgecomb, with Contributions by Mohammed M.A. Ahmed, Çeto Ozel

Lao Folktales
Wajuppa Tossa with Kongdeuane Nettavong, Edited by Margaret Read MacDonald

Princess Peacock: Tales from the Other Peoples of China
Retold by Haiwang Yuan

The Singing Top: Tales from Malaysia, Singapore, and Brunei
Retold and Edited by Margaret Read MacDonald

Polish Folktales and Folklore
Retold by Michal Malinowski and Anne Pellowski

Mongolian Folktales
Retold by Dashdondog Jamba and Borolzoi Dashdondog, Edited by Anne Pellowski

Far North Tales: Stories from the Peoples of the Arctic Circle
Translated and Retold by Bonnie C. Marshall, Edited by Kira Van Deusen

Tales from the 7,000 Isles: Filipino Folk Stories
Dianne de Las Casas and Zarah C. Gagatiga

Pachamama Tales: Folklore from Argentina, Bolivia, Chile, Paraguay, Peru, and Uruguay
Retold and Translated by Paula Martín, Edited by Margaret Read MacDonald

Tibetan Folktales
Haiwang Yuan, Awang Kunga, and Bo Li

Tales from the Arabian Peninsula: Folktales of Bahrain, Kuwait, Oman, Qatar, Saudi Arabia, the United Arab Emirates, and Yemen
Retold by Margaret Read MacDonald and Nadia Jameel Taibah

INDEX

Page numbers in **bold** indicate an "About the Author" entry.

ABOUT THE EDITOR

DR. MARGARET READ MACDONALD, folklorist, storyteller, and children's librarian, is author of over 65 books on folklore and storytelling topics. Work as a Fulbright Scholar in Mahasarakham, Thailand, connected her with storytellers throughout Southeast Asia. She continues to travel frequently to this area and has facilitated publication of folktale collections by friends from Indonesia, Laos, Malaysia, Thailand, and Singapore. Invitations to tell stories in Brazil, Cuba, and Argentina brought her friendships with tellers from these countries, which resulted in more folktale collections for the Libraries Unlimited World Folklore series. She has visited 95 countries and has shared her stories in Argentina, Austria, Australia, Bangladesh, Belgium, Bahrain, Brunei, Brazil, Cambodia, Canada, Chile, China, Colombia, Costa Rica, Cuba, Czech Republic, Denmark, the Dominican Republic, Egypt, Finland, France, Georgia, Germany, Hong Kong, Hungary, Iceland, India, Indonesia, Italy, Jamaica, Japan, Kenya, South Korea, Kuwait, Laos, Luxembourg, Malaysia, Mexico, Myanmar, the Netherlands, New Zealand, Oman, Poland, Puerto Rico, Qatar, Saudi Arabia, Singapore, Spain, Swaziland, Sri Lanka, Switzerland, Taiwan, Thailand, Uganda, and Vietnam.

MacDonald's Folklore PhD thesis was a motif-index of children's folktale collections. This became her *Storyteller's Sourcebook: A Subject, Title, and Motif-Index to Folklore Collections for Children* (Detroit: Gale Research, 1982). Her storytelling technique books include *The Storyteller's Start-up Book* (Atlanta: August House, 2006) and *Teaching with Story: Classroom Connections to Storytelling*, coauthored with Jennifer MacDonald Whitman and Nathaniel Forrest Whitman (Atlanta: August House, 2013).

MacDonald's Web site is www.margaretreadmacdonald.com.